I Wish I Didn't Quit: Music Lessons

Inspire Your Child With Tips From World Class Musicians

Nathan Holder

HOLDERS HILL
PUBLISHING COMPANY

First Printing, 2018

ISBN 9-7819997530-0-9

Holders Hill Publishing Ltd

www.iwishididntquit.com
@iwishididntquit

Contents

Dedication

In loving memory of
Richard Holder & Ezra Husbands

To Alexander, Eden, Josiah & Khaliah
*If you ever want to know why I didn't quit,
look in the mirror.*

Foreword

'I wish I didn't quit'. Music teachers hear adults say that all the time. Why is there such an epidemic of quitting?

As a kid, I was lucky enough to have access to music classes in school. But like most kids who enjoy such access, I quit as soon as I was able. I'm unusual in that I found my way back in, persevering to the point that I became a professional musician, and then a music teacher (and a teacher of music teachers). Most musicians I know in the worlds of rock, hip-hop, electronic dance music or other pop styles have a similar story. So if we love music so much, why did we quit in the first place? It isn't just the professionals and dedicated amateurs. Most young people love music. So why do so many of them abandon making it?

Sometimes life gets in the way. Sometimes it's an issue of time, or money, or logistics. But very often the issue is motivation. It's easy to blame kids for laziness or lack of discipline. But that wasn't the case for me, and it isn't the case for most people. Too often, we quit because we don't like the music we're studying, or we don't know what we're working toward, or we're being controlled too tightly, or not tightly enough. Music is hard. But we make it harder when we teach or learn it the wrong way.

What makes a musician? It isn't 'talent'. Like Nathan, I don't believe that such a thing exists. Anyone you see with 'natural' musical ability is really someone who has just put in the hours. It takes three things to make a musician: means, motive, and opportunity. Nathan deals with the motive part. How do you power through the sometimes boring and tedious aspects of practise and study? Being pushed by authority figures like parents and teachers might work for a child, but adolescents don't respond well to it, and as an adult you're responsible for pushing yourself. The motivation has to be internal and genuine.

The good news is that there are a lot of paths up the mountain. There are as many ways to teach and learn as there are musicians. If one method isn't working, that isn't a reason to give up; it's a reason to find another path. It helps getting up the mountain if you can see the top, and if you can see it clearly. In fact, the mountain has many peaks, and you can choose the one you want to aim for. Nathan helpfully lays out a variety of ways to be successful as a musician. Fame, wealth, or critical adulation are fine, but they are not the only peaks to aim for. Playing well enough to express yourself and have fun might be a more meaningful (and certainly more attainable) form of success. Nathan describes people who succeed without even being particularly great musicians: as producers, songwriters, music business figures, and even standup comedians.

Instrument technique, music theory, notation, audio engineering, songwriting, improvisation - these things are complicated, and it takes a long time to get good at them. But they aren't even the hardest parts of becoming a musician. The biggest challenge is mastering your emotions. You need to develop the confidence, the drive, the sustained attention, the honest self-assessment and reflection, the methodical effort, and the ability to be simultaneously disciplined and relaxed. These are skills that have to be learned just as much as playing in tune or keeping good time. This book can help you learn them, or teach them, or support someone else in learning them. And that's a big deal, because those skills don't just help you succeed at music. They help you succeed at life. Nathan wants to help you find your path and figure out how to walk it. The rest is up to you.

- Ethan Hein (Doctoral fellow in Music Education at New York University)

Introduction

I was having regular piano lessons up until the age of 12 when boredom got the better of me. I grew tired of the time it took to go to a lesson every week. There were many occasions when I played the tunes I wanted to, rather than practise what I needed to. There were times when I didn't practise and was told off by my teachers. There were good and bad performances. There were performances which I practised hard for, thought would be perfect, but left me feeling discouraged when they fell short of my expectations. I saw other piano players and wished that I could play like them, but nothing I did ever sounded as good. I wished that my teachers could show me what I wanted to learn, but if I'm honest, I didn't know all the options available to me. I wanted to be inspired. I wanted to be an amazing piano player but I had no idea how to actually get there. Fortunately after I quit having lessons, I started to teach myself how to play chords when I was about 15, and formed group with some friends. I was able to progress and this knowledge of harmony became useful when I started to learn how to improvise on the saxophone.

A few years later, I moved to Hamburg, Germany and started to work as a keyboard player, playing for a few different bands in the city. I don't remember the first time it happened, but often after I'd play a show, people would express to me that they used to play an instrument, but they quit. I could relate to many of the reasons why they decided to quit, and started to wonder how many people have the same experience of starting to learn an instrument, becoming bored, quitting and later on regretting that decision.

This book contains many ideas, situations and opportunities which I have personally experienced, thought about and learned from many musicians over a number of years. This is by no means the definitive text on how to raise a musical child, but it is a guide which will help you to think about how the choices you make and the attitudes you have, can affect your child's musical journey.

I've purposefully avoided too many references to different studies and academic texts for a couple of reasons. First of all, these texts and articles are available online, and if you are reading this, the chances are that you already have read an article or two about how learning an instrument can improve a child's academic and social skills. Secondly, I wanted this book to be more personal. I wanted you to read about real life experiences rather than sifting through dense academic language and theories. The musicians quoted in this book are people who have inspired me personally, and I was fortunate to have detailed conversations with some of them about different aspect of their musical journeys.

I encourage you to skip backwards and forwards throughout this book. The process of learning an instrument

‰

is often not linear, so why should reading about it be! Find the sections that are relevant for you and your child, and don't worry if some sections don't apply to you now - they may one day.

If there is only one thing you take away from this book, let it be this: In any activity your child pursues, help to give them as many opportunities and insights as possible so they never have to say,

'I Wish I Didn't Quit'.

- Nathan Holder

1. Sound Familiar?

Olivia is a typical 8-year-old. She enjoys playing with her toys, although she will happily spend hours playing games and watching videos on her mum's phone. She is doing well in school, often gets told off for talking too much, and still thinks that the boys in her class are yucky. She has an older brother named Timothy, who has weekly drum lessons and plays in a band at their school. Olivia likes playing with her brother's drumsticks when he is not looking, often hitting anything in sight, sometimes including Timothy. When she cannot use his sticks, she will clap, dance and sing along to many of the songs that she hears at school, and that her parents play at home. She is surrounded by music from the 70's and 80's like Stevie Wonder, Pink Floyd and Queen, with her parents often telling her that, 'They don't make music like this anymore'.

Tired of telling Olivia to stop hitting her brother with his own drumsticks, her mother thinks that maybe if Olivia channeled some of that extra energy into having music lessons, she may not only become very good, but learn a few skills which she may be able to use later in life. After discussing with her husband and considering the prospect of having two children armed with drumsticks, she asks Olivia if she would like to learn how to play the piano. Olivia's eyes sparkle and she nods furiously, picturing herself playing her favourite songs in front of her school-friends and family. After finding a teacher and making all the necessary arrangements, Olivia's mum drives her to her first piano lesson with a smile on her face. She is happy that she has been able to provide these opportunities for her children, especially as she was not able to learn an instrument when she was younger. Her parents could not afford music lessons, and placed more value on subjects like maths, English and science. She had known better than to ask her mum for the violin lessons she had craved.

At her new teacher's house, Olivia fidgets at the piano and glances nervously at her mum, who encourages her to sit still and listen to the teacher. Olivia looks at the piano, which is bigger, wider and shinier than any of the keyboards at school, and tentatively touches the ivory keys when her teacher asks her to. The lesson goes well, with her teacher asking Olivia what she can already play, then showing her a little tune and flipping through a book for beginners, telling her what they will try to learn in the following weeks. After leaving the lesson, Olivia's mum asks Olivia if she likes her new teacher. Olivia responds with a smile, telling her that she is really excited about starting piano lessons. Olivia's mum is quick to remind her to do exactly what her teacher says, and that these lessons will cost time, money and energy. To encourage Olivia further, she talks to her husband and they decide to buy a new keyboard for Olivia to practise on at home.

Olivia and her brand new keyboard are inseparable for the next few weeks and she makes rapid progress, learning some note names and attempting tunes like *Freré Jacque* and *Twinkle Twinkle Little Star* with one finger. Even though Olivia's mum is happy that Olivia is learning, sometimes listening to Olivia use different instrument sounds, drum beats and playing the same songs over and over again, can be quite frankly, annoying. She often quietly complains to her husband and friends, telling them that she cannot wait for Olivia to get better so she can play more complicated classical pieces. She knew that Olivia would not be selling out concert halls within 6 months, but she did not realise how annoying all the practising could be. Subsequently, Olivia is told to practise her keyboard with headphones on, to save headaches and inevitable arguments.

As time passes, Olivia starts to play and practise less and less. She plays the keyboard with minimal enthusiasm and often presses her whole hand on the keys to make noises, rather than picking out individual notes. When asked how her lessons are, Olivia's answers start to change from a detailed description of what she learned to, "It was fine". Instead of practising the things her teacher told her to, Olivia tries to play some of her favourite songs, but they do not sound anywhere close to how she thinks they should. Sometimes, she skips through the book she is working through with her teacher, and only 3 or 4 song titles get her excited about progressing. The lines and dots on the pages are starting to look more and more complicated, which leave her wondering if she will ever get through the book and move on to something that she really enjoys.

Olivia continues to attend lessons, but she starts to feel more and more frustrated. She wants to learn how to play the latest songs that all her friends are singing, but she's been told by her teacher to practise a tune named *Cartwheels* for the past month. Olivia asks her mum if she can play something different, but her mum tells her to listen to what her teacher says and in time, she will be able to play other songs. Olivia huffs and puffs, and throws the odd tantrum at home.

As time goes by, her teacher senses Olivia's frustration and asks her what is wrong. She has clearly not been practising properly, as they have been working on the same tune for a while. Even when she turns up to lessons, her attitude is very different to the girl who seemed so full of excitement and energy when they started. After talking to Olivia and understanding how bored she is with the songs she is learning, they agree to work on a song Olivia loves, which brings that sparkle back into Olivia's eyes.

Olivia continues to progress and after a couple of weeks, she is able to play a simple version of a pop song in a school concert, which makes her parents so proud of her achievement. They have seen their little girl progress from banging on her keyboard, growing frustrated and crying, to being able to play in front of a small audience in spite of her nerves. Through their beaming smiles and wild applause, they start to imagine how good she could be in 10 years if she keeps up this rate of progress. After the concert, they tell Olivia how proud they are of her and echo her school music teacher, who keeps praising her obvious musical talent.

Olivia has always been very active and as she gets older, her involvement in other after-school activities begins to grow. She does gymnastics, swimming and extra tuition every week, in addition to her piano lessons and homework. It gets more and more difficult to practise for the 30 minutes a day her teacher tells her to. She must prepare for exams and tests throughout the school year, not to mention Easter, summer and Christmas holidays, which often interrupt her progress. Even when Olivia has the time to practise, if her mum does not say anything, she has the tendency to conveniently forget. Sometimes, Olivia is so tired because of school and other activities, that she finds it hard to concentrate during piano lessons. Sometimes, when her mum tells her that she must practise after dinner, Olivia takes a long time to eat her food. Sometimes, she would rather eat broccoli than practise her instrument.

Her teacher enters her into a grade exam and as the date approaches, her teacher starts to worry that Olivia is not making the necessary progress needed to pass. This frustrates her teacher, as he knows that she has the ability to do very well. He tells Olivia's mum that she needs to practise much more than she has been, or else she will fail the exam. Olivia's mum is very angry after hearing this news. She usually takes Olivia to lessons and makes sure the teacher is paid without having too many conversations about Olivia's progress. She trusts that Olivia is doing what she needs to do at home to pass, especially as her teacher has made it clear to Olivia what needs to be practised. In a bid to make sure Olivia passes, she threatens to take away TV time, and stop Olivia's other activities until the exam is over. "Don't make me waste all this time and money Olivia", her mum frequently scolds.

Through tears and tantrums over the next few weeks, Olivia practises as much as she can, and actually passes the exam with ease. Olivia tells her parents that she wants to quit playing but they refuse to let her. The songs that she really wants to learn were put on hold while she got ready for the exam, and now the vision she had of herself singing and playing her favourite songs has become a distant dream. She has another small performance at school which does not go as well as the last one, which further dents her diminishing confidence. She spends her practise time playing songs she is familiar with and wants to learn, instead of practising the songs and scales she is supposed to learn to pass the next exam. Her parents seem unsympathetic and unable to understand the change in Olivia's attitude. Her homework seems to take longer and longer each day; sometimes she would rather do her homework than practise her instrument.

After further arguments and ultimatums from her teacher, Olivia's parents decide that Olivia can take a short break from piano lessons for a while, and concentrate on gymnastics which she really enjoys. That short break turns into 3 months. Then 6 months. 9 months. A year passes. Then 2. 3…

Now in her early 20's at university, she attends one of many open-mic nights in the area with a group of friends. After the show, she meets some of the musicians and starts talking with the keyboard player, telling him that she really enjoyed his playing. He asks Olivia if she plays an instrument, and she replies that she used to take piano lessons, but now wishes that she didn't quit all those years ago. In the time since she took that 'short break', she has seen videos of Beyoncé's female band The Sugar Mamas, Chick Corea, and André Rieu playing live on stage. She has seen various pianists not only playing classical music but pop, r&b, and other genres that she really enjoys to listen to. As she leaves the open-mic night, she is full of regret. She wonders how good she could have been if she did not quit all those years ago. Although she is not even 25, she feels as though it is too late to ever learn how to play an instrument properly. She now understands why her mum pushed her hard and vows that if she ever has children, she will encourage them to learn an instrument and not let them quit like she did.

Does any part of this story resonate with you? If your child is learning an instrument, chances are that many elements of this story will unfortunately sound very familiar. You may have even been through some of those same experiences yourself. As a parent, you understand that learning an instrument is a valuable skill and a big opportunity that some children may never have. You know that it takes time and dedication to learn how to play an instrument well. You want your child to have fun and become engaged in musical activities, but it is not going as well as you thought it would. Sometimes it seems that no matter what you do, your child would rather do anything other than practise their instrument. You know that if they quit, they will regret that decision in the future. Do you ever ask yourself?

- What happened to the enthusiasm they had in the beginning?
- Why don't they understand the opportunity I have given them?
- Am I putting too much pressure on my child?
- How can I stop my child from quitting?

This book will give you many suggestions and tips from musicians and music industry professionals who know what it takes to learn an instrument. The insight they provide will hopefully cause you to think differently about how learning an instrument really works, and what you can do to help. Whether you learned how to play yourself, or this is your first foray into the world of musical instruments and lessons, you no doubt have many ideas and questions about what it really takes to learn an instrument. Many people believe that learning classical music gives the best musical grounding possible. Others believe that certain instruments are better to start on than others. Are there enough reasons for learning a musical instrument outside of improving maths and English skills? Are there ways to keep your child engaged and motivated to practise their instrument?

The aim of this book is to help you make sure that Olivia's experiences don't repeat themselves with your child. This book will explore the different scenarios, problems and misconceptions that can stop your child from reaching their potential, equip you to deal with ups and downs, and help your child along their musical journey.

So, let us start at the beginning. What expectations do you have when your child starts their musical journey?

2. What Do You Expect?

Expect everything so that nothing comes unexpected. - Norton Juster

When you first decided to commit time and money for your child to have music lessons, what expectations did you have? It may be a difficult question. Do we really stop and consider what we expect to see or hear from a child, before they start learning an instrument? If we do, how realistic are those expectations? If a child is offered a place at a top school or academy, most parents will naturally expect different things from them in the future, than if they attended an average school. Expectations of a child can range from being accepted to a world famous university, to taking over the family business, learning a practical trade or finding a passion and pursuing it, irrespective of income. No matter how high, low or specific some of the expectations you may have for your child are, your reactions to their behaviour, results, successes and failures will often be based upon those same expectations. What you expect from your child, their music teacher and even from yourself in the beginning, will affect how you approach the ups and downs that come with learning an instrument and music lessons.

Even if you are a musician, the chances are someone else will be teaching your child how to learn a musical instrument. This means that apart from your own expectations, there are the expectations of the teacher and your child which will need to be understood and managed over the course of their music lessons. Understanding these relationships, can be key in helping your child to succeed.

<u>The Relationship Triangle</u>

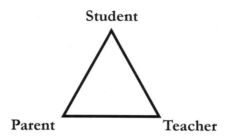

When you, as a parent, decide to give your child lessons, like it or not a relationship forms between you, the teacher and your child. The relationship you have with your child outside of this is separate but can overlap, especially if lessons are not going so well! In this model, you form the base alongside a teacher, to support your child on their musical journey from different sides and in different ways. In an ideal situation, parents and teachers communicate well and form a strong relationship, with the sole aim of helping a child to learn their instrument. Having unbalanced relationships may result in a child not feeling supported by a parent or teacher, a teacher not feeling supported by a parent, or a parent not feeling supported by a teacher. When there isn't enough support from teachers or parents, children can find themselves isolated from their parents, teacher or both. When everyone's expectations are aligned, or at least understood, the relationships can begin to work more effectively for a child's benefit.

So, now we know what the main relationships involved in music lessons are, what are some of the things they may all expect from each other?

<u>Parent(s) → Child</u>

Parents provide music lessons for their children for many different reasons, some of which have nothing to do with what a child wants for themselves! Some parents who were not able to have lessons when they were younger, can sometimes push their children into learning the instrument that they wanted to learn years ago. Others know that to get into a good secondary school, being active in a particular sport or playing an instrument, may give their children an advantage over others. There may be a need for another activity that a child can participate in after school because of work or travel commitments. Some may have read articles and watched news reports about how a musical education can have a positive impact on a child's maths and English results. Many parents however, decide to give their children lessons because their child asked, or showed a sustained interest in a particular musical instrument.

Whatever the reasons are, the fact is that music lessons for children often mean energy, time and financial commitments. If you are giving lessons to your child, you will naturally have expectations; after all, no one wants to invest in anything, without seeing either short or long term results. What expectations may parents have of their children?

• To try their best

The fact that you are reading this book, means that you not only care about your child's musical education but you are determined to make the best out of your investment and to help your child succeed. While using the word investment may sound strange in this context, if you saw maximum effort from your child, you would most likely continue to invest into their future. Seeing your child trying hard and enjoying the learning process, no matter what the results are, is what many parents really want to see. Many parents will provide lessons on the condition that if effort is not being shown, the opportunity will be taken away.

• Be the Ant, not the Grasshopper!

Do you regret not working hard enough when you were younger? Have you ever said to yourself, 'If only I had studied harder/read more/listened more/partied less, I may have achieved more?' The earlier you start learning a particular skill, the chances of success increase. This idea is shown in possibly no better way than in Aesop's fable entitled *The Ant and the Grasshopper.*

The Ant is working hard, storing food for the winter when the Grasshopper passes him on the road and laughs at him, telling him to relax and to enjoy the summer. The Ant replies that he must work now, because a time is coming when he will not be able to gather food. He must do as much as he can before the winter comes. The Grasshopper mocks the Ant and continues to relax in the sun for the rest of the summer. When the winter comes, the Ant is safe and warm in his house, when there is a knock at the door. The Grasshopper, shivering outside in the cold with no food and shelter, asks for help, regretting the fact that he had not prepared diligently for the winter.

When you provide music lessons, you expect your child to be like the Ant and to work hard, in the hope that they will reap the benefits in the future, and not have any regrets about wasted time, money or energy. The Grasshopper represents those who were given the chance to learn an instrument, but squandered the opportunity and wished they didn't quit.

• To see steady progress

Unless the main reason for your child to have music lessons is to have fun and occupy time, you will expect to hear and see improvements. After all, if your child has been playing the same piece in the same way for 6 months without progressing, that's a problem, right?

• Have fun!

Even though learning an instrument involves hard work, it can still be enjoyable. There is a higher probability that your child will continue learning, if there is an element of fun incorporated into their lessons and other musical activities. Plus, you would probably rather see your child smiling while playing their instrument, than hearing sobs in between notes, and angry looks in your general direction.

• To be attentive in lessons
How can you learn without paying attention?

• To pass exams
Many parents view passing exams as an important part of learning an instrument.

• To become bored
Even though this is a negative expectation, some parents will expect this to happen. It may well do, but if you expect this to happen, be careful. The expectations and attitudes you have, may influence your child more than you realise. Ask yourself and your child's teacher if there is anything you can do to prevent it from happening.

• Do everything the teacher says
Especially if you have no musical knowledge, you may expect your child to listen and absorb everything a teacher says, no matter how crazy it may sound.

• Tantrums
Learning an instrument often involves processes that many children do not like. If you expect this to happen, what would

trigger a tantrum? Is there anything you can do to prevent one?

- **To have a future career in music**

Why spend all that time and money on lessons and instruments, if your child grows up to work in a non-music related industry?

- **Not to quit!**

<u>Child → Parent(s)</u>

Even though many young children may not be able to tell you exactly what they expect, you can usually tell by their reactions if something unexpected occurs. Just imagine your child's reaction if any of the following happened:

- You forgot to take them to a lesson.
- You forgot to pick them up from a lesson!
- You forced them to go to lessons when they did not want to.
- You put too much pressure on them.
- You forgot to buy them equipment they needed.
- You took away their toys and made them practise.
- They felt that you were not being patient with them.
- You did not notice when they were excited about a new piece or something they learned in a lesson.

Many of these things may sound trivial, but this goes to show that there are many things that children expect from you once you give them the opportunity to learn an instrument. You as a parent, are much more important to the process of learning an instrument than you may have originally thought. Even though you may feel as though paying for lessons is enough, there are additional expectations placed upon you which are essential for your child to feel supported and understood.

Parent(s) → Teacher

A teacher who can understand and manage a child's expectations, can have a profound impact upon a child's musical journey. Not every teacher will be the right for every student. Perhaps the first thing to consider, is what you are looking for in a teacher and what you expect from them.

At the beginning of any professional relationship, we often have an idea about what we may expect from the other person, even if those things are never actually spoken about. We do not need to ask a waiter if the cutlery has been cleaned, or if the plumber needs a wrench when they come to fix your sink. When paying for a service, we expect certain things to be done, accounted for, or automatically considered. What are some of the expectations you may have of your child's music teacher?

- **Musical proficiency**

Who would want a music teacher who could not play the instrument they taught? Not many of us! You may expect to hear a teacher play and be amazed by their level of skill. You may hope that one day, your child will be able to play at, or better than the level of their teacher. You want to be able to say to your child, 'If you do what your teacher says, you could be as good as them one day'. A teacher who can play their instrument well, will often have a good amount of knowledge specific to that instrument, as well as general musical knowledge to pass on to your child. Depending on what you and your child want, you may not feel as though an internationally-recognised pianist is the best fit for your 6-year-old, but a music student attending a local university may be better suited to the level and energy of your child.

- **Relevant experience**

So, you want your child to learn how to play classical music on the flute? When you are looking for a teacher, you may expect a teacher to have a reasonable amount of experience in the classical music field. That experience could include qualifications, notable performances and perhaps their own recordings. You may also expect them to have had previous teaching experience, even if it is not extensive. You may expect a teacher to share personal experiences and to give your child some insight into what being a professional musician can involve. A musician who specialises in live performances, may concentrate more on sound and ear training as opposed to reading notes and theory. A more academically minded teacher may focus more on technique and theory, as opposed to expression and ear training. Having an idea about the direction you want your child to go, can make finding a teacher with the relevant experience much easier.

• **To develop an appropriate relationship with your child**
Often, teachers can develop close relationships with their students. That may be brilliant for communication, but becoming too friendly may result in a teacher becoming too lenient and a child becoming too relaxed.

• **To be able to motivate your child**
As we will discuss later in this book, there may be times when your child is no longer motivated to practise their instrument. You may expect a teacher to have the ability and flexibility to help your child get through difficult moments.

• **To be organised**
A teacher should know what was covered in the last lesson and have all the necessary equipment for your child to learn.

• **Have relevant connections**
You may expect a teacher to have knowledge of any music clubs or bands which may suit your child in your area.

• **Have a plan**

To have clear methods to be able to help your child make consistent progress.

• **To be reliable**

No last-minute cancellations or poor time management.

It's fair to say that these examples are all reasonable expectations to have from a teacher. No one would want a teacher who does not motivate, inspire, or respect you or your child. In trying to create a firm base and good support for learning, communication with your child's teacher can help you to understand your child in a way you may never have before. Where a school teacher may have up to 30 children in a class, a music teacher, after spending one on one time with your child, can potentially share observations which might help you to better understand your child's learning processes and creativity. Good communication will allow important information to be shared between you and a teacher, instead of relying solely on your child acting as a messenger (which can potentially cause a few problems). You may have had the experience of your child forgetting to give you their parents evening letter, to tell you that it is their turn to bring something in for show-and-tell, or about non-uniform day. Some children may try to avoid practise, by saying things like, "No, my teacher said I only have to practise for 15 minutes a day" (instead of 30 minutes) or, "No, I just have to practise this piece. No scales or anything".

The relationship between you and your child's teacher is key, as it can provide the stability a child needs to not only learn an instrument, but to express themselves and learn the meta-skills which can aid them in other areas of life (see chapter 8). It is this relationship which provides consistency in scheduling and the equipment needed for learning, but also the one which can create the most friction and frustration for your child. If you and a teacher are not able to understand each other's expectations, things can go quickly and horribly wrong.

<u>Teacher → Parent(s)</u>

Even though many private music teachers may not work in a school, many are professionals who have personal, as well as professional expectations of what music lessons should be like. These expectations will differ from teacher to teacher, so it is very important to have an idea of what your child's teacher may expect from you. Some of these include:

• To respect their opinion
Unless you are an experienced musician, a teacher will often expect you as a parent, to comply with their opinions and methods about practising, instrumental repair or learning materials. Some teachers choose to teach outside of schools, so that they can have autonomy over how, when and what is

learned. Others teach outside of schools because of their own schedules. They may not want someone else telling them how to do the things that they feel they have more knowledge about. Even if you are an experienced musician, a teacher will still need to feel as though they are being listened to, and not undermined as a professional.

• Punctuality

Some teachers may have lessons scheduled one after the other, and it can be difficult for them to teach your child for 30 minutes if you turn up 10 minutes late. Constantly showing up late can impede your child's progress, as 5 minutes lost at the beginning or end of each lesson will soon accumulate.

• Supervised practise

Teachers will often set exercises, pieces or scales for students to do at home, and (especially for young children) expect parents to make sure they do them. That may not mean that you need to sit and scrutinise every time they play their instrument. By keeping an eye and an ear out for certain techniques and trying to identify mistakes, you can support your child at home. Music lessons can also be an opportunity for you to learn about music yourself, and to actively participate in another aspect of your child's life.

- **Encouragement and discipline**

During difficult times, teachers will expect parents to help encourage their child. Whether that comes in the form of treats, sweets or kind words, parents ultimately know how to encourage their children better than their teachers. The same goes for discipline. If a child fails to meet expectations, many teachers will expect their stern words to be reinforced by a parent to help to keep a child focused.

- **Make sure all equipment is provided**

It can be frustrating for a teacher if a child shows up to a lesson with a book, bow, reeds or strings missing or broken. They may have planned a lesson in advance but then have to adjust because something has been forgotten.

- **To give enough notice when cancelling lessons**

Music teachers have lives too, and some may have children of their own. Knowing at least 24 hours in advance if a lesson needs to be cancelled or rescheduled, is a reasonable expectation. Some teachers may even charge you for the cancelled lesson if they are not informed in time.

- **For parents not to show much interest in what their child is learning**

Even though it is very negative, many teachers do not expect any real participation from parents. It does not mean that a teacher will not be able to do their job, it just means that a teacher may feel isolated. A teacher may start to drastically lower expectations if they know that their student receives little to no support at home.

- **To be blamed if a child is not making progress fast enough**

There will always be an expectation for progress to be made, but a teacher can only do so much. Parents are also responsible for the progress their child makes, and failure to recognise this, can result in teachers feeling unsupported. This is another reason why it is important to have expectations stated clearly, and updated regularly.

- **To be paid on time**

What happens if these expectations are not met? As you can imagine, a teacher may start to make less and less effort preparing for lessons, and pay less attention during the lesson itself. It may be unfair to the child, but many people lose interest and give less effort in a job because of changing or unrealistic expectations. When expectations are not clear, that key relationship which supports a child may start to crumble.

<u>Children</u>

Children have expectations too! What they expect from music lessons, may be the biggest obstacle they face along their musical journey and your plans for them. What are some of the things they may expect from their music lessons?

• **To impress their friends**
Many children want to be able to share their skills on social media in the hopes of getting likes and follows.

• **To get help when needed from parents and their teacher**
Sometimes children won't verbalise when they really need help. They may just show signs of frustration or disinterest, and subconsciously expect an adult to pick up on those signals.

• **To see themselves improve**
It can be frustrating to feel as if progress is not being made fast enough. Many children may need help managing their expectation to see instant improvements.

• **For lessons to be fun**
Some children may have friends who really enjoy their lessons and expect for their experience to be the same. Others may have seen professionals enjoying themselves playing live, and not realise the time and effort that went into making those performances special.

- **For lessons to be boring**

Some children don't like the idea of having music lessons. There are many ways to help them understand the value that learning an instrument can bring, as we will explore later.

- **To start by learning how to read music notation**

Learning to read notation is often one of the first things that children learn in their lessons. However, some children simply don't want to learn to read music. Those lines and dots can be very confusing at first, and especially frustrating if they don't enjoy the pieces they are being told learn.

- **Not to listen to any music**

Sadly, some teachers teach their students without encouraging them to listen to music. If listening to music plays no part in learning an instrument and their music lessons, many children can start to lose interest.

- **Not to feel pressure**

Your child may feel as though this is an activity they should enjoy, rather than one in which they are expected to meet deadlines and show progress.

- **Learn new music**

A child may expect to be taught the latest popular tunes that they like. They may expect their teacher to be open minded and not just stick to playing one particular genre of music.

- **Not to have their parents sit in during lessons**

Music lessons may be the one of the only moments in a child's life where they feel as though they can genuinely be themselves, away from the demands of school and peer pressure. There is potential for children to feel restricted if their parents sit in on every lesson, watching and analysing their every move.

Expectations will vary from child to child. Some children expect to be playing Beethoven's *Moonlight Sonata* after a few weeks. Some expect that it will take years before they can play anything that will impress their friends. Some may even expect never to be any good at all.

Children will often claim that they can do anything after seeing a footballer's silky skills or hearing an evocative saxophone solo. When we think that we can play something we hear, in that moment we unknowingly place expectations on ourselves. By thinking, 'I could do that, it sounds easy,' we place our perceived natural abilities above the hours and hours of practise it might take to play what we heard. Playing along to *Seven Nation Army* on air guitar with White Stripes guitarist Jack White, is really easy and a lot of fun. Playing it on a real guitar however, is not as straight forward. After the first few attempts to play, we may feel disappointed or frustrated when our first attempt at playing that famous guitar riff doesn't go so well. Sometimes, an instrument or a piece of music looks so impossibly difficult, that we do not even attempt to play it. We may see a professional musician play, and quit learning an instrument before we even start, when we realise the amount of time needed to accomplish what we just heard. Often, we quit before we really even try.

Especially at a young age, we rarely have expectations of how long it will take, how often we will get things wrong, how frustrated we may become, or what we can do with a skill once we have learned it. Perhaps one of the keys to making the most out of music lessons, is to help a child to be realistic about the things they should or should not expect to happen. That does not mean that children should not be told to dream big! It just means that by having some understanding of their own, their parents' and their teachers' expectations, when children eventually do start to learn an instrument, they have a clearer idea of the successes and failures that may lie ahead.

If everyone has different expectations and ideas about how music lessons should be, how can you reconcile all of these differences to make music lessons the best possible experience? It is all about communication.

Communicating and sharing your expectations with a teacher, can allow any existing thoughts, fears and wishes to be clear, and will hopefully help to avoid future conflicts. Having an open conversation with a teacher and your child, can give all involved a clear idea about the direction their music lessons will take. Boundaries can be set and explained from the very first lesson, which can also give you more insight into what kind of teacher you have in front of you, and how your child will respond to their methods.

The long term expectations that a teacher may have, need to match up to the long term expectations you have for your child. If you want your child to become a world-famous violinist and a teacher does not have the right expectations of you or your child, that dream may never be realised. Without having an individualised plan for a child, or at least an understanding of what it takes to get where your child needs to be, realistic expectations cannot be made or met effectively.

Do you want your child to win the BBC Young Musician of the year award, or to have fun and learn? To get into a good secondary school, or be able to contribute musically to your community? To have something to upload to YouTube or to fulfil a dream that you had for yourself years ago? There are vast differences between each of these goals and to achieve any one of these, different expectations are required. Having an understanding of these expectations, can help a child have the best learning experience possible.

Principle #1 - Learn To Manage Expectations

Help your child to have a good understanding of where they want to go, and help them write down the expectations they have for themselves and others (including yourself). Teachers, circumstances and opportunities may come and go, so update as time goes by and communicate as much as possible.

♫ ♪

3. Who Said Music Was Easy?

Divide each difficulty into as many parts as is feasible and
necessary to resolve it - Rene Descartes

There are many challenges that will need to be thought about when your child starts having music lessons. Some challenges will need to be spoken about with their teacher, and others will need you to understand them before these challenges become bigger issues.

Schedules

Author Karen Berger writes:

'I had a student once, who showed up for piano wearing his karate uniform, after eating dinner in a moving car; after piano lessons, he was headed for night skiing. No wonder this little 6- year-old vomited at the piano. I felt nauseated just listening to his schedule.'
(Berger, 2016)

Many children today are over-scheduled. Tennis on Mondays, extra tuition on Tuesdays, football on Wednesdays, dance classes on Thursdays and swimming on Fridays. It may sound crazy but many children take part in 3-4 different activities a week on top of their homework, household chores, and a social life. While exposing your child to a range of different activities and experiences can have many benefits, it must come with the understanding that with more time devoted to other activities, less and less time can be devoted to practising their instrument. Sure, it may be convenient to do 15 minutes of practise before eating dinner or before going to school in the morning, but will those 15 minutes be the quality time a child may need with their instrument? Can a child really focus and learn, when the smells from the kitchen are making their stomach growl, or feeling tired and dreading the prospect of a long day at school? Even the day chosen to have a music lesson can be important. Having a lesson on a Monday may result in cramming practise in on a Sunday, whereas a lesson on a Friday may encourage practise on the weekend, where the previous lesson is fresh in a child's memory.

The question to ask yourself is this: Do I invest in one or two activities that my child can really excel at, or 4-5 activities to try and develop a well-rounded child? Are you raising a jack of all trades or a master of one? The advantage of being able to provide a child with many different activities, can turn out to be a disadvantage, if they fail to become really good at one particular skill. The less time devoted to learning a skill, often the slower the rate of progress will be. To put energy into many different activities, means that expectations may have to be adjusted, relative to the amount of time spent learning an instrument. Perhaps the disadvantage some parents have in being able to only provide resources for one activity, (music lessons for example) can become an advantage, as a child will only have to focus on learning that instrument in addition to school work. If a music teacher understands that your child has a hectic schedule, they may also lower their expectations, set less homework, and expect not to see steady progress. You may want to see rapid progress in all activities but sometimes that is just not realistic!

That being said, learning an instrument as a child can influence someone later in life to pick up an instrument. The late Wayman Tisdale was a part of the gold medal winning 1984 USA basketball team, and played for 12 successful years in the NBA. After he retired, he picked up the bass guitar he had learned to play in his father's church when he was younger, recorded 8 albums and saw his 2001 release *Face to Face* reach No.1 on Billboard's contemporary jazz chart.

Musical Interests

As we will see in later on this book, your child's musical interests and instrumental lessons do not have to be mutually exclusive. If you know that your child likes One Direction (as much as you may not), why not let their teacher know? Sure, you may prefer to hear your child play a Chopin nocturne, but perhaps the right teacher can find a way to link the two. If not, then there are many activities that you can do to help learning an instrument become more interesting for your child. Watching bands like Aston on YouTube, who specialise in creating classical covers of pop songs including, *Smells Like Teen Spirit* by Nirvana and *Viva la Vida* by Coldplay, can help children open their minds to endless possibilities.

Personality

Unfortunately, many teachers have to find out about tempers or bad attitudes on their own, when a parent could have warned them beforehand. Knowing about a student's personality, can allow a teacher to adapt their teaching before any bad behaviour happens. Teachers can be better prepared for whatever may happen, especially if they are alone during a lesson. This also goes for good behaviour, or anything/anyone a child really likes or admires. Any additional information about a child can help a teacher connect with them, and make music lessons more enjoyable.

Exams

For many parents, taking music exams are the definitive way to show and record progress. Just like getting a grade in school, a music exam can give an indication of the level that a child is playing at. If you do not know the difference between *staccato* and *sforzando*, *treble* and *bass clef*, or *major* and *minor*, how else can you gauge the progress of your child apart from talking to their teacher?

While there are many advantages to taking exams, there are many people who do not believe that taking them is a real indication of musical ability. Some teachers and professional musicians believe that because these exams test students on 3 or 4 pieces and a set group of scales, they do not necessarily encourage a broad musical education. Children can be at risk of just learning how to pass an exam, rather than a full understanding of music and their instrument. However, exams do give a definite structure to learning, and help to give a sense of achievement for children, teachers and parents. Taking exams can help students to:

- Work towards a deadline.
- Develop short and long term goal setting techniques.
- Become familiar with their instrument's repertoire.
- Learn to handle pressure.

Young children may not understand straight away, but passing an exam demonstrates skills that potential employers often value. Working towards deadlines, independent learning and coping with pressure, can help in many different situations that children may find themselves in the future.

School Lessons

Music lessons in school can have enormous benefits, but it is important to understand that they can have their limitations too. Music lessons in school are often a very good introduction to learning an instrument. Most lessons will last between 15-30 minutes, usually because children may have to leave regular school lessons, or have a reduced break time in order to fit them in. As a result, peripatetic music teachers may have low expectations of the children they teach, as they know they may have up to only 30 minutes a week with them, and minimal or no contact with their parents. Sometimes lessons can be in groups, which means that a teacher's attention may be divided between 2 or more children.

Having 30-minute group lessons also means that it can be difficult to get into detail. If a child plays a woodwind instrument, they may have to assemble their instruments carefully and tune up - we all know children can be very slow if they are not totally motivated to do something! String players have to tune their instruments and maybe apply rosin to their bows. Brass players may have to oil valves. Students may arrive late for lessons and that time cannot be made up, as teachers often have to stick to a strict schedule. Sometimes students simply forget about their lesson and do not turn up! Ideally, children should arrive a few minutes before to get set up, but it often means missing valuable time in other subjects.

Lessons in school also usually involve playing in ensembles, which means that individual or group lessons can often be focused on what needs to be learned for a school performance. There are many benefits for children who experience music lessons in this way. Not only can it help to increase social skills, but there may be some elements of competition with children wanting to make sure that they don't make any mistakes in front of their friends, or try to play better than the person sat next to them. Playing in school concerts can teach children about stage presence, give them confidence and to learn how to deal with the pressure of playing in front of strangers.

<u>Continuity</u>

Many parents expect to be with the same music teacher for years and years. Some teachers expect to be with the same students for years and years. Why? Is that always a good thing?

The benefits of having a consistent teacher can include:

- Good knowledge of their students' schedules.
- Solid relationships can develop.
- Expectations are more likely to be clearer over time.
- The wants and needs of the student will be better understood.

Are there any advantages in not having a consistent teacher? Andrew 'The Bullet' Lauer is an internationally respected bass player, who currently lives in Germany. He believes that having many different influences can help to mould a well-rounded musician. He says:

'I think it's important to have different teachers. If I am teaching someone for more than a year I will tell them to find another teacher. If you have one teacher for too long you will sound exactly like them! Go and learn from other people!'

There can be negative effects from having one teacher for a long time. It can result in a student mimicking the mannerisms and even the bad habits their teacher has. It can also limit the influences a student is exposed to by having the same teacher for years. So why not learn from a few different teachers?

For younger children this may be more difficult, as having regular lessons in the same place with the same person, gives the stability needed for the initial stages of learning. This does not mean that young children cannot benefit from many influences outside of their regular lessons. By thinking of a teacher not as the stereotypical older authoritarian figure but as a musical influence, having many different influences can give a student a broader musical experience. As we go through this book, we will see how some of the most successful musicians in the world have learned, and how many of them often have the experience of learning from more than one 'teacher' on their journey.

The Balancing Act

It is important to examine your motivation, knowing that if you are really placing your wants and needs above your child's, they can grow to hate the very thing you want for them. Many people never had the opportunity to learn an instrument, and now that they are able to provide lessons for their children, they do so. They know that the more skills you have, the more job opportunities may become available, the more money can be made and the more secure a child's future can be. You may start trying to live through your child, expecting them to behave like you think you would have if you were given the same opportunity. Is that fair?

London bassist Jerry Logan, has played for artists such as Wretch32, Izzy Bizu and Michelle Williams (formerly of Destiny's Child) during his career so far. His father was the main reason why he became a professional musician, even though it was not always fun.

'When I was young, my dad used to lock me in my room with a guitar and tell me to practise. I hated my dad for that. I used to cry and refuse to practise. Now I am a professional bass player and I am so thankful that my dad forced me to practise. I wouldn't do that to anyone but fortunately it worked out for me.'

Many parents have had a heavy hand in their children's successes. The father of classical pianist Lang Lang, told him to commit suicide after he failed to get into the Central Conservatory of Music when he was just 9 years old. If you did learn an instrument when you were younger, you may want your child to experience the same things that you did, including the same books, the same repertoire or even the same teacher. This approach comes with its own expectations, especially if you were able to achieve a high level of musicianship. You may want your child to be a classical violinist, but maybe they are gravitating towards hip-hop and the drums instead. Should you then force your child to follow in your footsteps?

Even though Bruce Springsteen is one of the most decorated and highest selling musicians of all time, only 1 of his 3 children have followed him into the music industry. You, as a parent, cannot ultimately predict or force your child into doing what you want them to do. You do however, have a certain amount of control over the environment your child grows up in, which will have a great impact upon the direction they decide to go in.

How Can I Help?

With speaking about all the different expectations, and challenges, the question of the musical parent arises. How can you make sure your child is practising correctly? How can you make sure regular progress is being made? Outside of certificates and teachers' feedback, the only real way is to know for yourself. You can use your child's music lessons as your own chance to learn. Being able to listen to your child practise and comment on what you hear, can reinforce what your child is learning in their lessons. By being in contact with their teacher, sitting in on a few lessons, or even just using Google, you can learn certain words and phrases your child needs to remember for specific pieces, tunes or scales. Instead of generic comments like 'that sounds good', phrases like 'remember more staccato in this section' or 'don't forget the up and down bows', not only provide practical musical advice, but can help your child feel as though you are actively engaged in what they are doing.

Principal #2 - Know What You're Up Against

There will be many different challenges that you will face, but it's important to have an idea what might happen. Prevention is better than cure.

4. Was Mozart Just Born With It?

Sheer effort enables those with nothing to surpass those with privilege and position - Toyotomi Hideyoshi

Every parent loves to think of their child as being talented. At some point, many parents have seen or heard their child do something and thought, 'Wow...My child is a genius!' If a child says their first clear words at 8 months, who wouldn't dream of them receiving degrees from Oxford and earning six or seven figures salaries? Those lines, recited so well in the school nativity play, could be Academy Award acceptance speeches to proud parents. That goal your son scored against you in the park, has you dreaming of him winning a Ballon D'Or and representing your country at the World Cup. However talented you may think your child is, only a few are ever regarded as prodigies, and fewer of those go on to have long and sustained careers. There are many children who may not be regarded as talented, but who achieve success through persistence and hard work. What does it take for a child to be regarded as a prodigy? Does precociousness guarantee future success? Should you worry if your child shows no sign of musical ability?

Prodigies are generally defined as children under the age of 18, who are performing at the level of an accomplished adult in a complex field. Some musical prodigies of the last 10 years include Jay Greenberg (Composition), Joey Alexander (Piano), Tony Royster Jr (Drums), Cory Henry (Organ) and Grace Kelly (Saxophone).

Grace Kelly began playing classical piano at the age of 6 but switched to jazz and wrote her first song aged 7. She recorded her first CD as a jazz saxophonist at age 12, and has since recorded and/or performed with prominent musicians such as Phil Woods, Dianne Reeves and Harry Connick, Jr. Although she is only 26 years old, she is the youngest ever 3-time Downbeat Alto Saxophone Rising Star winner, as well as having won awards all over the world for her compositions and soloing ability. Where did this ability come from? Even her father Bob Kelly does not know:

'I don't know where that comes from,' he said. 'With the saxophone, once she picked that up, after the first couple of months, she could play songs... She was so entranced by the instrument, we had to tell her to go to sleep.' (Leopold, 2016)

Where did that passion come from? Are prodigies born, or are they made? Let us try to answer these questions, beginning by examining the most famous prodigy of them all.

Wolfgang Amadeus Mozart

Mozart has long been regarded as the prodigy of all prodigies. He started composing at the tender age of 5 and died aged just 35, but not before completing approximately 600 compositions and securing his place as one of the most influential figures in the western classical tradition. Since then, the search for the next Mozart has led to many children being pushed at younger and younger ages to become accomplished pianists, violinists and any other 'ists' you can think of. International competitions are held annually to showcase the best young talent, with many children being touted as future stars and musical innovators. When we see a child performing at an adult level, our immediate reaction is not only to be amazed at their level of skill, but also to wonder how good that child could be in a few years with the right guidance and exposure. The question is, how did the Mozart develop those skills in the first place? Was he just born a genius? Let's see if we can explain how Mozart became Mozart.

Mozart was born in 1756 to a wealthy family in Salzburg, Austria, the youngest son to his father Leopold and mother Anna. When Leopold started teaching Mozart's older sister Nannerl in 1758, Mozart's curiosity was ignited:

'He often spent much time at the clavier [an early form of piano], picking out thirds, which he was ever striking, and his pleasure showed that it sounded good.... In the fourth year of his age his father, for a game as it were, began to teach him a few minuets and pieces at the clavier.... He could play it faultlessly and with the greatest delicacy, and keeping exactly in time.... At the age of five, he was already composing little pieces, which he played to his father who wrote them down.' (Deutsch, 1966)

As Mozart continued to compose and improve, his father stopped his own work to dedicate more time to further instruct his son. The family made several European tours during Mozart's young life, which meant that he met many respected musicians, such as J.C. Bach (the son of the more famous Johann Sebastian Bach) and Josef Mysliveček, who would both become important influences for him.

So, who was Mozart's biggest influence? Arguably his sister Nannerl! Even though his father was an accomplished musician, it seems as though his sister starting to learn the clavier, sparked Mozart's interest. Younger siblings often copy much of what older siblings do, so it is no surprise that Mozart took an interest in the clavier when his sister started to play; not before and not many years afterwards. Leopold was one of the best composers in Vienna at the time, which meant that Mozart was being instructed and influenced by someone with a very high level of musical skill. Leopold was also an accomplished violinist who played in an ensemble for the ruling Prince-Archbishop of Salzburg. Not only that, but Leopold book *Versuch einer gründlichen Violinschule*[1] reveals that he was not only an accomplished musician, but an extremely knowledgeable teacher. The opportunity to tour around Europe, was only afforded to a very small percentage of people in 1750's Austria. To have access to a harpsichord or clavier in the 18th century, was a privilege many of us living in developed countries in the 21st century cannot fully understand. The fact that Mozart had access to one at home,

---

[1] Translation: A Treatise on the Fundamental Principles of Violin Playing

shows what an important role his family's socio-economic status played in his success.

As we start to break down the idea of talent and prodigies, we start to see that there are many more factors involved in the making of great musicians, than just being born with a supposed musical gene. Earliest influences, environments, socio-economic status and a hard work ethic, are all factors which can determine the path of a young musician. The support that Mozart had, especially from his father, was extremely important for his development. For many other young children, is parental support the determining factor?

<u>George Frideric Handel</u>

George Frideric Handel was born in Halle, Duchy of Magdeburg (modern day Germany), in 1685. Unlike Mozart, his father was against the young Handel's involvement in music. He banned Handel from playing musical instruments of any kind, as he intended for him to study Law.

Nonetheless, the young Handel was somehow able to obtain a small clavichord, which he played on at night, while the rest of his family were asleep. By the time he was 13 years old, he had persuaded his father to allow him to take lessons, and played for Frederick I of Prussia. He also learned about harmony and counterpoint, as well as learning the oboe and violin from Friedrich Zachow, the man who preceded J.S. Bach as the organist in the former Dom in Halle. Handel went on to be considered as one of the greatest composers of the Baroque era. His compositions such as *Zadok the Priest* (1727) and *Messiah* (1742) resulted in the honour of him being buried at Westminster Abbey when he died in 1759.

Here we have an example of a child who was forbidden to play an instrument, but found a way to satisfy his curiosity and learn for himself. There cannot have been too many children in the 18th century who were able to essentially order a clavichord, and hide it in a room in their house where their own father could not find it. If Handel was from a poor family, what are the chances he would have been able to access a clavichord at all? How does a child with no teacher and no family support, reach a level of musicianship to persuade his father to allow him to study with Friedrich Zachow?

Even though the stories of these two musical giants are very different, we can see that it takes more than just the support of a parent like Mozart's or the determination of Handel to produce a prodigy. Are you disappointed that your child is not considered as a prodigy? There is no need to be. There are many children who have gone on to be successful musicians, or found joy in playing casually, who were never prodigies or even regarded as very talented. What, then, is this thing called 'talent'?

It is difficult to define what talent really is. Talent cannot be measured, bought, stolen or sold. It is also totally subjective, which is often seen on TV shows such as *The Voice* or *X Factor*, where the opinions of the judges and the opinions of the audience can be very different! In recent years, these talent shows have shown us that there are many more talented people in the world than we may ordinarily encounter. TV and the Internet have given people a platform to showcase their talents, in the hope of being able to make a living from their passions and inspire others.

There are many videos on YouTube, Instagram and other social media platforms, of young children who exhibit a high level of skill and musical knowledge, playing and arranging music seemingly well beyond their years. The comedian Ellen DeGeneres, has seen increased interest in her show *Ellen*, partly because of her penchant for finding young talented children online, and giving them a chance to perform on her show. By recording and uploading videos online to sites like YouTube, families are directly supporting children, subliminally letting them know that their skills are worthy to be seen by millions of people. Recognising, cultivating and encouraging talent is an extremely important part of helping children to reach their potential.

Every Saturday, Stuart Kanneh-Mason used to take five of his children on a train from Nottingham, to their music lessons at the Royal Academy of Music in London. His daughter Isata Kanneh-Mason, reached the finals of the *BBC Young Musician of the Year* in 2014 and is currently a Sir Elton John Scholar at the Royal Academy of Music in London. Her brother and cellist Sheku Kanneh-Mason, won the *BBC Young Musician of the Year* award in 2016, becoming the first black recipient of the award. Despite Isata's undoubted talent, the dedication of her parents (who also happen to be accomplished pianists) is a significant reason why her dreams are en route to being realised. She says,

'My parents have always been extremely supportive of my siblings and I. Despite both of them either having jobs or being busy they always sacrificed their time to listen to our practise, take us to music lessons, competitions and concerts and give us really helpful advice. They know how much all of us love music and want to succeed, and so they have always been there to help make sure that we can achieve those dreams.'

Perhaps children who reach a high musical standard, achieve this by a combination of the ability to work hard, a certain socio-economic status, and the advantage of being surrounded by parents, teachers, siblings and friends who can encourage and help to facilitate musical growth. It has been well documented that the Jackson 5 did not have a relaxed time under their father Joe Jackson. Nevertheless, they became a successful group and laid the musical foundations for the then child star and future King of Pop, Michael Jackson. As hard working as they undoubtedly were, would they have been so successful if they weren't treated by their father so harshly? The Beatles weren't child stars or individually considered to be enormously talented in their youth, but after Allan Williams facilitated the chance for them to acquire residencies at clubs in Hamburg, Germany in the 1960s, they became arguably the most successful band of all time. Are prodigies and talented people born, or are they created? Whichever side you decide to take, it is clear that those musicians, talented or otherwise did not make it all by themselves.

The challenge that teachers, parents and carers face, is to spot any signs of talent and to encourage it to flourish. Before any lessons take place or instruments are bought, there are many things that you as a parent can do to nurture musical talent. You can sing with your child in the car, before bedtime, or even during bath time. You can clap rhythms while watching TV commercials or rhythmically hit pots and pans in the kitchen. All of these activities can help engage a child with music, from as early as a child can clap their hands and make sounds. Having music playing in the house and showing your child album covers and artwork, talking about musicians and by you playing an instrument yourself (however badly), can also help your child to take their own interest in music. There are many documentaries which profile famous musicians and bands, which include interviews and performances that you can watch together. By providing instruments for children to play on whenever they want to, children will automatically start to try and reproduce the sounds and songs they have heard on CDs, on the radio or at school. From keyboards to kazoos, tambourines to trumpets, instruments of any kind around the house can encourage your child to experiment and learn.

The 24-year-old London-based musician, Jacob Collier, grew up with many different instruments in his home. He has received praise from music aficionados and leading figures in the music industry such as K.D Lang and Quincy Jones, the latter of whom claimed, 'I have never in my life seen a talent like this' (Jacob Collier, 2016). His arrangements of popular songs like Stevie Wonder's *Isn't She Lovely* and *Don't You Worry 'Bout A Thing*, as well as his debut album *In My Room*, showcase not only his vocal arrangements, but virtuosity on a variety of different instruments. The videos he has self-produced, edited and uploaded, have amassed over 19 million views on YouTube, and earned him a place to study at London's Royal Academy of Music. Would it surprise you to know that his mother Suzie Collier, is a professional musician who has received an ARAM for outstanding services to the violin profession by the Royal Academy of Music, and conducts the Chamber Orchestra at the Royal Academy of Music Junior Academy?

Many people think that if they have a talented child, providing them with music lessons is all that is needed for their child to flourish. Sending them to lessons and buying the best instruments possible are all positive actions, but perhaps the key to raising a musical child is you. The passion you have for music (or not), the kind of music you listen to and the places you may go, can have more of an impact than you may realise. If you show no interest in music beyond listening to your favourite rock bands, the chances are that your child may reject much of the classical music that is often taught to beginners in private lessons and in schools. The musical surroundings of a child and the attitudes they are exposed to, are just as important as finding a good teacher or buying a good instrument.

Multi-Instrumentalists

Multi-instrumentalists are often regarded as more talented than those who only play one instrument. Is that a fair assumption to make?

In recent years, the availability of video editing software has allowed many musicians to upload videos of themselves playing different instruments at the same time. Search for the name Hamilton Hardin on YouTube, and you will find a video of what you may think are 6 men playing a bebop version of *The Smurfs* theme tune. In fact, Hamilton plays the piano, guitar, tenor saxophone, bass guitar, trumpet and drums all in the same video. Whether he is playing keyboards for Dave Koz or drums for BWB, Hardin has played different instruments for and with some of the top musicians in the world. What does he think of his musical abilities?

'I don't think the ability to play multiple instruments is as contingent on talent as most people think. Time allocation and a thoughtful systematic

approach with how one's practise time is spent is vital. Setting long and short-term goals, preferably with the added insight of an instructor, helps in the quest to target specific areas of weakness. And the weakest of areas can be transformed into one's greatest asset with time. But the drive to spend that time, in my opinion, is the gift from God.'

So he wasn't born able to play all of these instruments? There's hope for us all! Although Hamilton calls his drive a gift from God, others may refer to it as grit or determination. Whatever you decided to call that desire, there is no doubt, that 'talent' alone is not enough. The systematic and disciplined approach Hamilton refers to when talking about practising these different instruments, is one of the main reasons why he can play all of these instruments at such a high level. The journey to learn all of these instruments took time. He first started playing the drums, then moved onto the piano. He picked up the saxophone in 6th grade and everything else started to trickle in over the years.

One of the keys to unlocking the 'secrets' of multi-instrumentalism can be found in how the different instruments are inter-linked. Instruments are divided into four different families: Strings, Woodwind, Brass, and Percussion. Take the brass family for example. Even though a tuba and a trumpet look and sound very different, those instruments have more in common with each other, than they do with a bassoon or a viola. The same goes with all other instrumental families. A piccolo and a clarinet have more in common with each other, than they do with a cello. The ability to play one instrument in a family, can help you to learn how to play other instruments in the same family.

Rahsaan Roland Kirk was one of the most unique and extravagant performers jazz has ever seen. He perfected the technique of circular breathing, and often played with two, or even three saxophones in his mouth at the same time. Looking at the instruments he played, we can see that they all belonged to either the woodwind or brass family - the soprano, tenor, manzello, strich (all different kinds of saxophone) and flute. There are many adjustments to make when switching from instrument to instrument including breathing, embouchure (how your mouth is positioned) and the key the instrument is in. However, music theory and the elements that make up music (e.g. rhythm, tempo) remain the same across all instruments. By gaining a good grasp of one instrument, other instruments over time can become easier to understand and play.

Musical talent may not be an attribute someone is born with like eye or hair colour, but it seems to be more to do with a child's environment and musical influences. What is undeniable however, is that hard work plays a large role in whether music lessons will help a child to achieve their musical potential. Even for children who are regarded as talented, if they do not practise and continue to learn, their level of skill and technique and will start to decline. The great Lithuanian violinist, Jascha Heifetz once said:

'If I don't practise one day, I know it; two days, the critics know it; three days, the public knows it.'

To practise every day requires commitment and good time management, not to mention the passion and drive to want to constantly improve. For professional musicians, the reasons for practising and improving may be motivated by finances, fear of competition or a love for learning.

Children who show a passion for music need to be supported by parents, grandparents, siblings or other mentors. The routine, guidance and encouragement needed to achieve a decent level of musicianship needs to be consistent for any form of talent to grow. Many of the top musicians in the world can all point to friends, family or teachers, who in some way encouraged them, and helped to shape their musical journeys.

So why explore talent and prodigies at all? It is about exploring the myths that surround these ideas and helping you to understand that no one is born a world class musician. Mozart, Handel and others, needed many years until they produced the music we now know them for. Even though Mozart started composing at age 5, we somehow assume that these compositions were groundbreaking feats of musical artistry. They weren't!

Many children stop playing an instrument because they feel as though they are not progressing fast enough.

They see other musicians and feel as though they weren't born with a musical talent. When they see musicians of a similar age who may sound better or be progressing faster, that can lead children to feel as though they will never be good enough. By understanding what prodigies, talent and the effect of hard work are, you can further support your child by giving them many more advantages along their musical journey than just finding a good music teacher and relying on their innate abilities. You can help them understand, like Hamilton Hardin, that there is no real substitution for hard work, taking risks and receiving support from family and friends. Whether it means you have to travel great distances like Stuart Kanneh-Mason, have many instruments in your home like Suzie Collier, or change your attitude like Handel's father, the influence you have on your child will contribute greatly to their success. These children showed that they had a talent, but it was their parents, who in many different ways, allowed them to flourish and equipped them for the rest of their lives.

Principle #3 - Hard Work Beats Talent

Talent by itself can only take you so far. Being aware of the many other factors that make great musicians what they are, can help you make the best decisions for your child and not rely on their 'talent' alone.

5. What Is A Musical Environment?

I believe that children are our future, teach them well and let them lead the way - Whitney Houston

Many studies, blogs and bartenders around the world have come up with different theories and suggestions about the effect music has on children. We have all heard theories such as playing Mozart to your unborn child will increase their IQ (Rauscher et al., 1997) or improve reading (SFGate, 2016), maths and English skills (Johnson and Memmott, 2006). While some of these claims may have elements of truth to them, we know that there are many maths geniuses incapable of singing in tune, and many famous musicians who are hopeless at maths. Some think that certain people possess a 'music gene' which gives them an advantage from birth. Some children are born into musical families and are surrounded by live music and instruments, while others grow up without music in their immediate surroundings, and are influenced by their school friends, an event or videos they watch. By understanding what has helped some of the top musicians in the world progress in their careers, we can begin to understand how a child's musical environment can influence their own musical journey.

Family

When we read about many of the most famous musicians in history, we discover that many had an early musical influence in their family. Whether it was a grandparent, parent or sibling, having a strong musical influence in their close environment gave them a firm musical foundation. Johann van Beethoven, the father of Ludwig van

Beethoven, was a singer who also taught the harpsichord and violin. The father of the 2001 National Medal of Arts and multiple Grammy winning classical cellist Yo-Yo Ma, was a violinist and music professor. Grammy Award winner and jazz saxophonist Joe Lovano, was exposed to jazz at a young age by his father Tony Lovano, who also played the saxophone. Grammy Award winning jazz drummer Terri Lyne Carrington comes from a long line of musicians; her mother and father played the piano and saxophone respectively, and her first drum kit came from her grandfather who had played with the jazz pioneer Fats Waller. Other famous musical families include the Marleys (Bob, Ziggy, Damien, Stephen, Rohan, Ky-Mani), the Coltranes (John, Alice, Ravi), the Shankars (Ravi, Anoushka, Norah Jones), Kuti's (Fela, Femi), and the Jones' (Hank, Elvin, Thad). Just as we saw in the story of Mozart, it is clear that having a strong musical influence at home, can give a solid foundation for the start of a child's musical journey.

Bassist Steven McKenzie grew up in a large musical family, some of whom have gone on to have successful careers in the music industry. Steve and his brother Josh Mckenzie (known as MckNasty) have both played for UK rapper Wretch 32, while their younger brother Labrinth, has had two top 3 UK singles and written with singer Ed Sheeran. His sister ShezAr is the choir director for the London based House Gospel Choir. What was it like for him growing up as a child?

*'My grandad is a pastor but he also sings, my mum was always in the
choir and my dad is a guitarist. My mum's sisters were also in a big
gospel group back in the day. My brother was constantly encouraging me
to play bass because he was a drummer at the time, playing for lots of
gospel artists. I was really interested in learning saxophone but there
were no more spaces for it. I refused every single time [he encouraged me]
until I heard the rumble of the bass teacher playing double bass down
the hall at school in year 9. That was it, I was hooked.'*

Being born into a musical family does not
automatically guarantee that a child will become a musician.
There are many people who have famous or accomplished
musicians in their family, but never followed that path, and
famous musicians who never had a strong musical influence
at home. The mother of 1989 Rock and Roll Hall of Fame
inductee and The Rolling Stones front man Mick Jagger, was
a hairdresser. Mick was expected to follow in his father's
footsteps and become a school teacher, not a rock and roll
superstar. Jazz pianist Brad Mehldau's father was a doctor,
while his mother stayed home to take care of the family.
From these examples we can see that even if you are not
musical, it does not mean that you cannot raise a musical
child. It just means that if your goal is to raise a musical child,
there are many more elements to consider than just giving
them music lessons. What are some of the surroundings that
have helped to influence musicians all over the world?

<u>Church</u>

Musicians who have grown up and played in churches, are amongst the most sought after musicians in the world. Many mainstream pop, r&b and neo-soul artists, employ musicians and singers who started their musical careers in churches. Spanky McCurdy (Justin Timberlake, Lady Gaga), Cory Henry (P. Diddy, Bruce Springsteen) and Robert Glasper (Kanye West, Jay-Z) to name a few, all started their careers playing for their local congregations, and are now recognised as some of the best contemporary musicians in the world. Britanni Washington is best known as a keyboardist in Beyoncé's all-female band The Sugar Mamas. How did she learn to play in church?

'I was six years old, and we had an old piano in our house. When my mom [was out of the house], I would dress up like Diana Ross and put the whole shebang on, like a show for myself, till someone caught me. They said, "You can be Diana Ross." But I said, "It sounds weird without the music, and I don't have anybody to back me up. So, let me just try to learn it myself." This is at six years old! So, I went to the piano and I played "Ain't No Mountain High Enough," and my mom heard me playing the song. She said, "God's given you a gift, and you have to use it." So, I went to church that Sunday, and I played [the song] at church. After that, I played every Monday, Tuesday, Wednesday, Friday, and Sunday at six years old. I got my first paycheck at seven. I was playing for their church for about 18 years.' (Roland, 2016)

Many church musicians often start playing from a young age, and are surrounded by more experienced musicians than themselves. They are given their own space to work in, and sometimes the instruments are provided for them (especially keyboards, drums and organs). They are expected to play in front of large groups of people every week, as well as be musically flexible and know a large repertoire of music. They have to be able to be spontaneous, and have the ability to follow and anticipate whoever is leading the service at any given time. Some church musicians are paid to play in church, and expected to attend rehearsals during the week. These elements and more, contribute to how many young musicians can reach a high standard of musicianship from within the church environment.

Are church musicians born with instruments attached to their umbilical chords? Do they all study music at the best institutions and learn from the best teachers in the world? No. Perhaps the reason why many become so successful, is because they have to play in a professional setting at least once a week, year after year, constantly being pushed to improve by more experienced musicians than themselves. Although many musicians have greatly benefited from playing 2 to 3 hours a week in church, is that all that is needed to become a successful musician? No. Are all church musicians incredible musicians? Of course not. The church environment is merely another environment which many musicians have been a part of, which has helped them to hone their skills by learning from others and from their own mistakes. You do not have to start going to church to create a more musical environment for your child. If you currently do attend a church, encouraging your child to play consistently with others can be extremely beneficial. If you do not go to church, don't worry! There are other environments which exist or that you can create, which your child can benefit from.

<u>School</u>

School is often the place where children have their first experience of a musical instrument. Many musicians were either given an instrument at school, or were lucky enough to have been able to choose what they wanted to play. A boy by the name of Benjamin was enrolled in free music classes at a local synagogue when he was 10 years old. While his older brothers were given a tuba and a trombone, Benjamin was given a clarinet. He went on to become known as Benny Goodman aka the 'King of Swing', and is regarded as one of the most influential American jazz musicians of the 20th century. Andy Brown was given a guitar by a teacher at his primary school, and has since gone on to have 6 singles in the UK top 20, as the front man for the band Lawson. These two examples give us a brief insight into what can be possible if a child is exposed to an instrument at an early age, regardless of perceived talent or precociousness. It is often in their formative years, where children are at their most inquisitive and receptive, that lifelong passions can start to form and grow.

Why do so many parents agonise over the schools they send their children to? As well as a school's previous exams results, general reputation and traveling distances, they are acutely aware of the influence that other children will have on their own. Many parents will not consider a school for their children if they see the possibility of negative influences from the other children, or if the area is notorious for violence, drug abuse or religious extremism. We all know that a child's musical tastes are often greatly influenced by their peers in school, and because children are usually put into classes regardless of background and culture, this means that many children may start to gravitate towards music that some parents may not approve of.

Depending on culture and taste, genres like hip-hop and heavy metal may have polarising effects on parents. Parents may not approve of the lyrics or the general appearance of some of today's most popular artists, but their children may love them. Many parents may prefer for their child to idolise someone like Lalah Hathaway as opposed to Cardi B, or Michael Bublé instead of Justin Bieber. The truth is, that children will be heavily influenced not only by the music itself, but also by the image of these superstars. They may start to reject the traditional images of concert pianists or cellists, and instead gravitate towards tattooed rap, rock and pop stars. Consequently, there can be an uphill struggle in trying to encourage a child to focus on a classical piece of music, which even their parents may not listen to, let alone their friends. Although much music education in school is still focused around western classical music, initiatives such as Musical Futures and alternative schools of thought, are shifting towards a learning by doing approach, which encourages children to learn through the playing of popular musics rather than traditional theoretical methods.

Church and school are just two environments which can help to shape and direct a child's musical journey. The environment within which a child grows up in and the music they are exposed to in their families, the places they go to and their friends, are all factors in how successful music lessons can turn out to be. While there is no formula to create a musical child, understanding where and how your child interacts with music on a daily basis, can be key. If parents and teachers have a greater understanding of the environments their children find themselves in, expectations can be tailored for each child, and achievements can be understood relative to each child's environment and musical interactions. Even siblings who grow up in similar environments are very different, which goes to show that even the surroundings we are born into and find ourselves in, do not ultimately determine how successful music lessons will be.

Music Is All Around Me

In his 2013 memoir entitled *Mo' Meta Blues*, Ahmir 'Questlove' Thompson details his upbringing as a child born into a musical family. His father was Lee Andrews of *Lee Andrews and the Hearts* and his mother was a member of the soul group, *Congress Alley*. In addition to growing up on the road and being on tour with his father, mother and aunt, at home he was surrounded by a vinyl collection he estimates of around 5,000 records. He writes that because his sister attended all-white schools, she brought home music which she (as one of the few black students) felt would help her to blend in. This music, in addition to the music in his father's record collection, helped him to become one of the most sought after drummers, producers and DJ's of the last 15 years. He has worked with the likes of D'Angelo, Amy Winehouse and Elvis Costello, as well as being the co-founder of the Grammy award winning band The Roots. He writes:

'I loved the way that music was the center of our house, though I think I knew even at the time that it wasn't normal. Something strange was happening at 5212 Osage; I was getting a Harvard-style music education in a Joe Clark, Lean On Me environment. If you take an inner city ghetto where there's crime and violence and drugs - and there was all that around us all the time - the last thing you think you're going to find is a family that's teaching its afro'd four-year-old son the

difference between Carole King's original 'It's Too Late' and the Isley Brothers' version...'. (Questlove and Greenman, 2013)

Unless you are already an avid record collector or iTunes junkie, buying and playing a lot of music to your child just because you want them to be an amazing musician, isn't all there is to it. There are many musicians who did not grow up around a lot of music, even some who did not grow up listening to the music they are now famous for. One of the key components in Questlove's musical journey wasn't just that he was exposed to lots of music, it was that he was encouraged to actively engage in listening to different kinds of music. His parents talked about music to him and as such, he was able to appreciate music in a very different way to many children his age. If you aren't a musical parent, you too can engage your child in music, by listening to a wide range of genres and talking about the music you like and dislike. Encouraging conversations about music with your child at a young age will not only improve their musical awareness, but also their linguistic and reasoning skills too.

Finding Your Place

'Watch the company you keep and the crowd you bring, Cause they came to do drugs and you came to sing' - Nas

In a bid to create an environment best suited to their ambitions, some musicians have decided to move far from home to pursue a musical career. Some musicians travel for miles just to be around others who are musically like-minded or more advanced than they are, while others emigrate to have more opportunities to play and earn money. Seizing opportunities, no matter where they are or how crazy the idea may sound, is often a part of many musicians' success stories. While some are prepared to move to a different continent or country for the pursuit of their art, others may not want to take such a risk, but will travel for a few hours just to attend a jam session or a concert. They know that being in those environments, surrounded by people on a similar path, may help them along on their musical journeys.

When it comes to children, moving country, changing social groups, habits and routines just to give your child the best possible musical education is not feasible for most parents. As popular and as important as music can be, core subjects like maths and English, often take priority unless your child is already regarded as a prodigy or very highly talented. The musicians who decide to make big changes to further their musical careers do it for themselves. They take their own risks, sometimes after finishing compulsory education and in some cases, even returning to an instrument they had quit playing years before. They may have realised that they can make a living from music, or decided to try and take their passion more seriously. Nora Bite is a jazz guitarist and entrepreneur who moved from Riga to London.

'I think it's been only less than 15 years since something similar to 'jazz education' exists in Latvia because it used to be 'forbidden' music back when it was part of the Soviet Union. When I moved here my priority and goal was to keep myself inspired and improve. Being surrounded by amazing jazz musicians everyday was a big inspiration for me and it just made me happy... I was out jamming nonstop for 2 years. The amazing thing about music is that it doesn't matter where you come from because we all speak in one language [and] that is the jazz language. That's the culture on its own.'

In trying to raise a musical child, putting people in their lives who can help them succeed is crucial. The right person at the right time, can help to inspire a child from afar, or personally guide them in specific directions. Just like professional musicians who will seek out the people and places they need to in order to advance musically, you can also find the right musicians relevant for your child to listen to, speak to, see in concert or watch online. If you want your child to be a rock musician, find rock musicians in your area and encourage your child to talk to, learn from and play with them. If you want your child to be a classical clarinetist, find the classical clarinetists! The power of the Internet is such, that if personal contact is not possible, by reading books or watching interviews given by the musician in question, a child can learn about their practise schedules, successes, failures and dreams.

Facilitate vs Dictate

'I never teach my pupils, I only attempt to provide the conditions in which they can learn.' - Albert Einstein

You may have dreams of your child playing a certain musical style or performing at famous concert halls, but aren't too sure how to help them along the way. Do you force them to do what you think they should? Do you leave them to figure it out for themselves? You may have experienced this dilemma already. There are some occasions when your child has come to you, excited after playing a piece they have finally made progress on, but at other times, you may have had to shout or cut privileges in order to get your child to practise. It may feel like the pressure you place on them will lead to them wanting to quit, but you may be aware that when you give your child freedom, they show little to no effort in progressing or practising. What now?

dictate - *to say or state (something) with authority or power*

Some teachers, instructional books and courses, often dictate to students what to do, when and how to do it. These rigid structures have their merits, but it seems that many of these methods were absent in the formative years of some of the musicians we have discussed already (especially the non-classical musicians). Even though Mozart received lessons from his father, the fact that Mozart could compose at such a young age, shows that his father realised that growth occurs when skills are practised. He could have easily told the young Mozart to wait until he knew more about theory and was a more proficient player before he started to write his own music.

Many children these days are encouraged to learn music first by reading (music notation) then by playing and finally writing. Traditional classical music courses and books are useful tools, but can often result in musicians lacking the confidence to improvise and be creative. Similarly, without these methods, many musicians can struggle to read notation and fail to understand basic music theory.

facilitate - *to help (something) run more smoothly and effectively*

The musical surroundings we have already discussed are ones in which learning is not necessarily forced. The family, school and church environments are organic in nature, not carefully regimented and static, with no certificates or grades to assess levels of skill. Some of these musicians were able to grow up in homes in which musical instruments were available to them at any time of day. The church environment offers structure, often provides instruments and contains people with a range of different musical abilities and ideas. In school, children are free to exchange music and learn from each other. At jam sessions, musicians are free to play jazz standards, popular songs or improvise on riffs, all within a relatively controlled environment. Those environments allow learning to be facilitated by trial and error, the exchange of ideas, and a wide range of abilities and tastes.

Brittani Washington did not end up playing for Beyoncé just because she went to church. She has toured the world with one of the most successful artists of all time because her parents allowed her to play in church, gave her responsibility from a young age and allowed her to learn from her own mistakes. With years of practise, sweat and occasional tears, many children matured into the musicians they are today. Even though they may be selling millions of albums and touring the world, they continue to find the right environments to help them grow further, and to help inspire others.

As we progress through the school system, we gradually learn how to work alone. From our work being marked daily in primary school, we are slowly given more responsibility. Homework is set for completion over a week, coursework over longer periods of time, and periods of study time and self-reflective exercises in higher education. One of the important skills learned from having music lessons is that from the very beginning, children have the chance to learn by themselves. If they are given instruments to play, music to listen to and the right people to ask their questions, the skills learned from those activities can serve children well in their futures, musical or otherwise.

As a parent reading this book, you know that music lessons are there, not so that a child will continue to take lessons for the rest of their lives, but so that they take the attitudes, meta-skills, experiences and ideas they learn, into every aspect of their lives. If your child does not become a professional musician, would you be happy knowing that certain skills were learned just from the process of having music lessons? In providing this opportunity, do you then try to dictate the pace of learning by setting targets and fixing rigorous schedules, or do you facilitate learning by encouraging self-exploration? Is a blend of both possible?

In her book *Battle Hymn of the Tiger Mother*, Amy Chua details her experiences as she pushes her two young daughters toward musical excellence. She assembled intense practise schedules at home, and learned the nuances of the pieces her daughters were practising, so that she could effectively pick out mistakes and reinforce techniques that they were being taught in their lessons. On family holidays abroad, she organised pianos so that her eldest daughter Sophia did not miss a day of practise. Her youngest daughter Louise, almost always travelled with her violin. Amy's efforts and her daughters' hard work, resulted in Sophia performing at Carnegie Hall while she was still in the 8th grade, and Louise receiving a statewide prodigy award and becoming the concertmaster of a prestigious youth orchestra at the age of 12. While Sophia took it all in her stride and acquiesced with the extra practise sessions and her mother's insistence on perfection, Louise started to rebel against her schedule and assumed trajectory. Her relationship with her mother fractured as she accused her of selfishly pushing her into music, without any regard for her wellbeing or happiness. Through tears and a very public argument in Moscow, Amy agreed to allow Louise to play the violin on her own terms. Even though Louise (nicknamed Lulu) did not want to quit playing the violin altogether, she offered a simple explanation for her rebellion:

"I don't want to quit violin," Lulu repeated. "I just don't want to be so intense about it. It's not the main thing I want to do with my life. You picked it, not me." (Chua, 2011)

Every child is different and that is why understanding what a child wants for themselves, can only help you as a parent, in collaboration with teachers or mentors, to facilitate or dictate what is needed for musical growth. Finding that happy medium can allow a child the freedom to explore, engage and question. Giving children the freedom to experiment and question established techniques and methods, can help them to better understand the music they hear all around them. Of course structure is needed, but perhaps allowing freedom of expression within that structure, can remove any feelings a child may have of being forced to have music lessons. An organic environment, where questions and experimentation are just as important as the consistent practise prescribed by a teacher, could be a way to ensure harmony. By creating a balance between facilitating and dictating, children can start to gain a greater understanding of what they are trying to achieve. By attending concerts, playing in church or just listening to music, a child can start to see how music applies to their lives, in and out of lessons.

In looking at the environments of many musicians, we can see how they are all products of their own conscious choices, or by the choices of the people closest to them. With the right environment, a child can become a world class performer, a good musician or enjoy playing in their own time, rather than become an adult who wishes they didn't quit. When those who can help to shape their environment make the choice to understand how to facilitate and dictate the learning process, anything is possible.

As a parent, there are many choices you will have when raising a musical child. By understanding the different ways successful musicians have achieved their dreams, you will hopefully gain a wider perspective, and understand the many different options available, so that you can make the right decisions for your child.

So far, we have looked at people who have been fortunate enough to have grown up with musical families like Steven McKenzie, and grew up in positive musical environments like Britanni Washington. In the next chapter, we will look at the hard work required when the initial excitement of starting music lessons begins to fade. Those moments when your child pouts and throws temper tantrums. Those times when they forget to practise all week. Those times when your child says they want to quit having music lessons. If you do not have a huge record collection, do not go to church, or are not able to pass musical knowledge on to your children, what can you do?

Principal #4 - Create A Musical Environment

Help your child to achieve their potential by surrounding them with music, instruments and people who will inspire and motivate them.

6. When The Going Gets Tough

I know I can,
Be where I wanna be,
If I work hard at it,
I'll be where I wanna be.
- Nas

In an ideal world, all children would find happiness and fulfilment every time they blew, strummed or hit their instrument. However, just like Olivia in the introduction, there will inevitably come a time when a child will need to be encouraged to continue. How can you, as a parent, do that effectively?

"If you practise now, imagine how good you could be in a few year's time?!" - Every parent ever.

How many times have you heard or even said something like that to your child? As well-intentioned as that statement is, the concept of delayed gratification does not come easily to children, especially if the time scale suggested is incomprehensible (a year to a 10-year-old, is a lifetime!). There are many ways that you can encourage your child to practise or play their instrument, and some of these methods can have a large influence over the rest of their lives. In Olivia's example, her teacher decided to teach her a song she already enjoyed and knew, which gave her something exciting and familiar to learn. Olivia's teacher connected the unfamiliar (the instrument) to the familiar (her favourite song) which resulted in Olivia's renewed enthusiasm, even if it was only temporary.

Opening a child's eyes to the experiences that playing an instrument can give them and how music can make us feel, can aid a child in finding happiness and realising the purpose behind practise and routine. If as a parent, you can help your child to feel as though they are a musician, rather than someone who is told to play an instrument a few times a week, your child may have a higher chance of fulfilling their musical potential. Encouraging your child does not have to be the main responsibility of their teacher. As we've seen so far, it is when all relationships are balanced, that parents and teachers can have the greatest impact on a child's musical journey.

Home

Having different instruments at home can encourage children to experiment with the different sounds instruments can make. Encouraging your child's experimentation can spark impromptu family jams and play-a-long sessions, which can help to teach children how to take turns and listen, as well as to develop fine motor skills. These instruments do not even have to be 'real', as James Poyser, keyboardist of The Roots remembers:

' my mother tells the story [that when] I was a little kid, I used to play with her knitting needles on pots and pans in the kitchen. ' (daily.redbullmusicacademy.com., 2014)

Even though having a sense of structure and schedule in practising is important, there also needs to be a certain freedom for creative exploration. In the same way that many sporting careers start from children playing football, basketball or cricket with neighbours and friends, the option of having instruments to play on at home, can spark a lifelong passion.

At home, you have the chance to facilitate your child's musical journey by giving them experiences that would usually require a lot of money and time. Watching live (or pre-recorded) concerts on TV or on the Internet, is another option you can use to expose your child to how live music can look and sound.

Many children often complain that they do not like classical music and become easily bored when presented with a classical piece to learn. Why is that? Perhaps it is because they very rarely listen to classical music or see it being played live. They may not have the experience of seeing a professional string quartet, play in a school ensemble or see contemporary artists, like Gregory Porter or Michael Bublé performing with a live orchestra. If the only time they are in contact with classical music or traditional orchestral instruments is during their music lessons, there can be no surprise that an Allegro by Hayden or a Beethoven symphony does not fascinate or excite. Chances are, none of their friends listen to Hayden or Beethoven, and the pictures of these men, wearing elaborate wigs, are sources of amusement rather than inspiration and curiosity.

In his bestseller, *How To Win Friends And Influence People*, Dale Carnegie suggests arousing an eager want in the person (in this case, a child) you want to influence. Carnegie tells the story of Stan Novak, whose son Tim did not want to go to Kindergarten. Instead of telling Tim to go to his room and stop complaining, Novak came up with another idea. He thought about the activities that Tim might do at Kindergarten and along with his wife and older son, started finger-painting together and having fun. Soon Tim wanted to join in, but was met with the response, 'Oh, no! You have to go to kindergarten first to learn how to finger-paint' (Carnegie, 1936). The next morning, where was Tim? Sleeping downstairs, not wanting to be late for his first day at Kindergarten.

Owning books on music and musicians can also spark a child's interest. The books may not be read often, but just by having books available for your child, it gives them the option to explore whenever they want to. Any visual art, such as posters, fridge magnets, paintings or sculptures can also form long-lasting memories for children. By providing children with options at home, you can allow them to explore and find the activities that excite them. Once you see what they naturally gravitate towards, it will help you to make decisions as to which instrument they want to learn, the style of music and the expectations you and your child will have.

<u>Concerts</u>

*There's nothing to compare to live music, there just isn't anything. -
Gloria Gaynor*

Even for an accomplished musician, practising scales
and techniques on their instrument can be a lonely process. It
requires hours and hours of sitting or standing alone,
repeating exercises, phrases and passages of music. Many
musicians practise to become more proficient in their
performances, so if they do not have any upcoming concerts,
practising can feel pointless. The same goes for children.
Practising for the sake of practising can make little sense,
unless they understand the whole context of practise and the
reasons why it is important.

Taking a child to a concert can help to put their
practise into context. To see musicians on stage with their
instruments, how the audience responds and the anticipation
and spectacle of the whole performance, can be an essential
source of encouragement and inspiration. For many children,
the only time they may see live music is on a screen, and for
those of us who have been to live music concerts, we know
that those two experiences are totally different. The
difference between telling a child that if they practise their
piano they could be as good as Jamie Cullum, showing them a
video of Jamie Cullum or taking a child to see Jamie Cullum
playing the piano live, should not be underestimated. Even if
you could attend a concert that their teacher is playing in,

imagine the awe your child may have for their teacher afterwards! Children can become more motivated and inspired as world renowned violinist Sasha Ki recognises:

'Going to concerts for young musicians is important for a few reasons. It can be a great motivation to practise more, to play better, and one day to end up on a big stage.'

For a child to see how musicians play their instruments, the various sounds, how much fun they may have on stage and to feel the energy of everyone involved, can be an experience like no other. For some people, going to a concert has even been a life-changing event. Children may be fascinated to see how the equipment is set up and taken down, the clothes the performers wear and lighting, which can give a child a wider perspective on what it means to be a professional musician. Seeing and questioning all of the different aspects that make up a concert, may inspire a child not only to take playing their instrument seriously, but can also help ignite an interest in fashion, dance or videography for example, as they start to understand what is involved in making the singer, instrumentalist or band not only sound good, but look good too.

To see and hear how musicians make mistakes and recover from them, is an aspect you will not often hear on modern records, and may not realise by watching videos. As much as a teacher may tell a child not to stop if they make a mistake, a child may not really have had much experience to see what that discipline looks like in reality. In school, they are told to start again if they make a mistake, or to stop and start a sentence again if they stutter while speaking. Musicians can make mistakes and laugh about them on stage, sometimes along with their audience if they notice what happened. The realisation that making a mistake does not mean that a performance is ruined, can help a child to continue to play confidently even if they make a mistake.

Sasha Ki also values the experience that comes from hearing musicians play live rather than listening to recordings:

'Every time a musician plays a concert, it will be different from the previous time, and the experience we share when we play is also different, so the impression will be unique every time. That's for example, why live performance is preferred to the CD.'

Going to concerts also gives you the chance to meet some of the very musicians you or your child may admire. Depending upon the venue and situation, many musicians are very open and willing to talk, share stories and encourage, especially if they know your child plays an instrument.

In seeing all aspects of a live performance for themselves, a child can start to think about ideas they may want to try, things they may have done differently, and even things which they did not like at all. As a parent, you have the opportunity to engage your child in these conversations, share experiences and help them to understand the world around them. These different perspectives gained by attending concerts, can help a child to discover their own musical identity, and hopefully help the music they play and their instrument become even more personal to them.

Listening

'We have two ears and one mouth so that we can listen twice as much as we speak' - Epictetus

Listening to music is another way to encourage a child to continue learning how to play their instrument. Unfortunately, when children are learning an instrument, listening is often one of the most neglected skills, especially in genres which focus on reading. How important is listening to music when learning an instrument? To answer this, let's look at the links between music and language.

World renowned linguist Noam Chomsky has suggested that we are all born with the innate capacity to learn any language, and that the languages we learn are the ones we are exposed to the most. Although no-one remembers how they learned to speak, the basic premise of learning a language, is the ability to hear. Most parents will be able to remember at what month their child said their first word, read their first words and wrote their name. It is no coincidence that those milestones often come in the order of speaking, reading and writing, but it's the ability to listen which is developed before we are born. Grammy award winning producer and multi-instrumentalist Marcus Miller illustrated this point by saying:

'Music is a language.... When you learned English, did anybody tell you about verbs and pronouns? Nah, you just started talking, you just started imitating your parents and your family and people around you and you learned how to talk. Six, seven years later then they started to teach you about verbs and pronouns; they teach you what you are doing right? Well [that's the] same with music. A lot of you guys learn how to play by your ear. That's a beautiful and natural way to play. What's the next step? Now you've gotta learn what you're doing.' (Clark, 2011)

Listening is a much more important part of learning an instrument than we often realise. Students are often first taught how to play a note, read another and play it, until enough notes are learned to begin to play simple melodies. Sometimes students may be given exercises asking them to draw treble or bass clefs with the notes they learn. The first few lessons usually include instructions on how to hold, clean and take care of their instrument properly. After all of these lessons, students can often read, write and speak (play), before they have a good idea of what their instrument can really sound like. Knowing the different articulations, dynamics and effects that their instrument can produce, often comes much later, when a child starts discovering music specific to their instrument for themselves, or the music they are playing becomes more and more complex (if they don't quit before then).

When we look at examples of successful musicians, they often knew and were inspired by people who played the same instrument they later went on master. Many of them understood how their instrument could sound and what it could do, and were able to replicate certain sounds before they learned to read or write music. They spent time listening and playing along to records, memorising passages and patterns; they imitated what they heard around them. The understanding of what other musicians were doing didn't always come straight away, but by constantly listening, the music slowly became a part of them. Hannah V is a London based producer, songwriter and keyboardist who studied at the Royal Academy of Music and has played or produced for the likes of Rhianna, JP Cooper and Stormzy:

'I trained to be a jazz musician, after I fell in love with jazz in my early teens. Part of the culture of jazz is studying the greats. Nobody could teach you more than the masters, so I would religiously pour over Miles, Coltrane, McCoy Tyner, Bill Evans, Chick Corea, Herbie, etc - all the greats. I remember for years and years just not 'getting' Coltrane's 'Love Supreme'. Then all of a sudden, in a crowded London tube, something just clicked in me and I was in a trance. It all made such sense to me. Maybe I just needed to live a little.'

Active Listening

To actively listen to music, means to concentrate intently on the different elements which make up a tune or a piece. It means listening to a piece of music and analysing anything from how many instruments are playing, to the chord structure of a particular section, to harmonic structures and recording techniques. We may be able to hear the difference between a piano and a trumpet, but actively listening over time, will allow you to hear the difference between a trumpet and a trombone, and some people can even hear the difference between different brands of trumpet. While some people are seemingly born with the ability to identify different notes from each other without a point of reference (perfect pitch), the ability to recognise harmonic progressions, riffs and timbres, can be developed over time.

If a young violinist listens to a lot of music played on the violin, they will eventually begin to understand the nuances of what their instrument can do, and the extreme sounds and timbres it can produce with the right techniques. The multi-phonics of Pharoah Sanders, the breathy tone of Stan Getz, the growls of James Carter and the vocal style of Kirk Whalum, all show the range of sounds possible on a tenor saxophone. Songs like Sam Smith's *Stay With Me*, Alicia Keys' *If I Ain't Got You* and John Legend's *All Of Me*, all heavily feature a piano, and are good examples of how to play pop-style piano music. An aspiring lead rock guitarist might choose to listen to the album *Appetite for Destruction* by Guns 'N' Roses or *Van Halen* by Van Halen, to hear when and how the musicians solo and use different effects and techniques.

Children can also start to understand how there is more than one way to play and interpret a piece of music. How violinists Itzhak Perlman and Viktoria Mullova might play *Winter*, from Vivaldi's Four Seasons for example, would be slightly different to each other, even if they read from exactly the same score. This can lead children to think about and develop their own style when they realise that there is no right or wrong way to play a particular piece of music.

Listening to artists who have seemingly effortless and total control over their instruments, like Hiromi Uehara or Steve Vai, can have an amazing effect on children. Many who like what they hear, will try to sing or play along on their instrument. When they do that, they will start to absorb different nuances of performance and musicianship, as well as the fulfilment of being able to play along with world class musicians. This process is called transcribing, the practise of which is regarded as extremely important by many musicians and educators. Listening and copying, is essentially what children do when they learn to speak, which shows how connected learning an instrument and a language really are. Even encouraging your child to play along with the theme tune to their favourite TV show or advert, is a great way to learn while having fun and being able to impress friends. By doing this, children may start to become aware of how different they may sound on their instruments compared to a recording. Whether a musician's timing is slightly off or the tuning is not perfect, by a child starting to hear these imperfections, they can start to understand that what seems to be perfect, may not always be.

Actively listening to music is not just about understanding technique and sound. It helps children to connect with the music they may be currently playing, never enjoyed, or are already passionate about. Trying to empathise with how a composer may have been feeling when they wrote a piece of music, a performer when they are singing or playing it, or how the music relates to them, can be key in helping children understand themselves and the world around them. This process can help children to express their own emotions, thoughts and feelings about music, which can aid their overall development with or without their instrument. Here's what Hannah V has to say:

Listening to records is fundamental to me. My career is very different now, I produce pop records, but the ethos is still the same. I learn as much from an Aretha Franklin record as I do from a Kanye West track. The genre of music doesn't really matter, I am drawn to the emotion. I analyse records on a technical level as well as the chord changes, the sound selection, the arrangement, etc. I make a mental note of things I discover and then don't really think about it anymore. At some point the new knowledge amalgamates with my existing skills without me even realising. So for listening to music, new and old, is not just essential for my work, it is essential for my soul! Ultimately, I am a music fan and a music geek - I don't think I will ever get bored of discovering a new artist/record!'

Passive Listening

Passive listening is our ability to absorb the sounds we hear around us subconsciously. In the same way that pre-natal babies start by recognising their mother's voice and as they grow, begin to recognise the voices they hear most often (father, brother, sisters), a child's ear will develop the more they listen to music.

Encouraging a child to listen to music is not difficult. Most people use iTunes or Spotify, which combined gives you access to over 70 million tracks. The challenge is to encourage a child to listen to different types of music, as well as music specific to their instrument. There are many websites which list the top 10, 50 or 100 albums or songs of all time, many of which could be a good place to start. By picking and choosing from different lists and listening to one new album a week for example, children can start to learn to appreciate music that they may not be familiar with. In the car, on the way to and from school, background music while eating or doing household chores. All of these are ways to listen to and absorb new music without your child feeling like you are taking over their lives.

There are examples all around us, to help challenge children's perceptions and expand their horizons. Miri Ben-

Ari released her fourth album in 2005 entitled *The Hip-Hop Violinist*, and featured songs by many prominent artists, such as Wyclef Jean, Lil'Mo and Twista. Her achievements to date are proof that playing a violin does not limit you to playing the music of Sevcík or Dvorák, and being a part of a classical ensemble. The late Raphael Ravenscroft is the saxophonist behind the infamous solo on the 1978 hit *Baker Street*, which is just one example that proves that saxophonists are not restricted to just playing jazz music. Without having this knowledge, a child may never know that they can play the bassoon in a jazz fusion band (Bela Fleck & The Flecktones), or the cello on a pop record (*Wonderwall* by Oasis). For example, it might open a child's eyes to know that Dr. Dre used violins and cellos in his song *Still D.R.E.*, which became one of the most iconic hip-hop tracks of all time.

Listening to a wide range of music can also give children more ideas if they decide to compose or improvise. Syndicated BBC Radio 6 DJ Gilles Peterson has this to say:

'Knowledge is power. The more you study about the music, the more reference you have to create your own thing.'

The Beatles famously travelled to India to learn from local musicians, and to incorporate new ideas and approaches into their music. They and other musicians realised that to not only appeal to a wider audience but to keep their music interesting, they had to listen to a wide range of styles from different cultures and eras.

Many musicians will specialise in one genre but will still play, enjoy and even record in others. Although Wynton Marsalis is best known as a jazz musician, he has recorded several albums of classical music, including *Baroque Music for Trumpet* (1984) and *Classic Wynton* (1998), on which he plays the music of Handel, Mozart and Paganini amongst others. He became the first artist to win a classical and jazz Grammy Award in 1983, showing his versatility and providing evidence that it is possible to be world class in different genres. By listening to a wide range of music, students can begin to understand that there doesn't need to be such wide distinctions between classical, pop or jazz.

Exposing students to a range of music can also help to eliminate the feeling that there is right and wrong music, or a right or wrong way to play. Artists and composers like John Cage, J-Dilla and Ornette Coleman are all examples of people who challenged musical conventions, by disregarding rules and introducing different concepts. Some of their music may not be played on conventional radio stations or be music that you want your child to play, like but these three men were all very successful, and not only influenced music, but culture. This may have the effect of steering children away from accepted conventions, and towards a more experimental and philosophical approach to music and sound. But after all, what is the aim of providing musical lessons? Is it to mould a child into what you want them to be, or to provide a solid knowledge base so that they can explore in whichever way they deem fit over the course of their lives?

Bands

Tomorrow's Warriors is a youth jazz collective based in London, currently under the leadership of Gary Crosby OBE. It has helped to develop some of the UK's top jazz musicians including Denys Baptiste, Shirley Tettah, Soweto Kinch and Nubya Garcia. Like playing in church, a band gives its members a chance to learn and write music, interact with others and perform. By being a part of a collective like Tomorrow's Warriors, young people can often develop deep musical and personal relationships, pushing and motivating each other to learn and succeed over many years. Leader of the band KOKOROKO and co-founder of the band Nérija, trumpeter Sheila Maurice-Grey has this to say about her experiences playing in Tomorrow's Warriors:

'It was having that constant place to go to where you learn new music and the fact that it was challenging music exposed me and pushed me in terms of the music I was listening to. So now all the things that were enforced and said by Gary Crosby I still use in whatever genre I'm playing. People like Moses Boyd, Binker Golding, Theon and Nathaniel Cross, Ruben Fox and Mark Kuvuma are all now professional musicians you can see out in the limelight within jazz or doing their own stuff. It was a great environment to be in'.

Many studies have been conducted into the impact playing in a band can have on young children. One such study conducted by J.D.Brown (1985) found that, '91% of non-band parents, 79% of non-band students, 90% of drop-out band parents and 82% of drop out band students agreed that participating in a band builds self-esteem, self confidence and a sense of accomplishment.'

Positive peer pressure can encourage children not to quit in a way that parents often cannot. Giving children a sense of community, will not only increase their chances of sticking with their instrument, but the people they meet through that experience may help them discover music that they wouldn't otherwise. There are many bands, orchestras and community groups who always welcome new musicians regardless of age and experience. Although there may be a membership fee for some of these, the dynamic of learning in a group, can be extremely beneficial for a child and a worthwhile investment.

Jam Sessions

'If no one ever hears it how we gonna learn your song' - Emeli Sandé

In a *TedxGabriolaIsland* talk entitled *Music as a Language*, Victor Wooten shares his personal experience of how he learned to play the bass guitar. From the time he was born, he was surrounded by his four older brothers who were a complete band, except for the fact that they did not have a bass player. Victor started his musical education by sitting and listening to his brothers play, until he was given a bass guitar - but only to hold. He was then given a guitar with two strings removed, which became his first bass guitar (a standard guitar has 6 strings, a standard bass guitar has 4 strings). He concludes his story by saying that because he learned to play the bass almost at the same time as he learned to speak English, he now looks at learning how to play an instrument in a different way.

As we are learning how to speak, we are surrounded by adults who often have total command of at least one language, and who talk using full sentences, proper grammar and varying ranges of expression. As children, when we make mistakes like saying 'llellow' instead of 'yellow', we are smiled at, hugged and told we are cute for getting the word wrong. We continue talking to and listening to adults (professionals) for years, until we can say what we want, when we want and how we want to. Those children who grow up with more than one language around them, learn those languages simply because they hear and copy the professionals (adults) who speak them. In music however, we are told as beginners that we are only allowed to play with other beginners, and that when we are good enough, we can play with the intermediate players and only then, advance to interact with professionals. Unlike learning an instrument, if we make a mistake while talking, we are not told to go to another room and practise speaking for half an hour every day until we get it right.

Mistakes are often ignored with adults understanding that eventually, a child will learn the correct way to speak. Why can't we learn music in the same way? Why aren't beginners encouraged to play with professionals from the very beginning? Why are beginners told that mistakes are bad?

By going to and playing at jam sessions, children can play with musicians who often have decades more experience than themselves. They can also try out techniques and tunes that they have been practising at home, but with the added pressure of playing with other musicians and to an audience. After attending a jam session, a musician may want to practise a tune to play at the next event, or talk to a musician who may be able to give them tips on how to improve. Mistakes are always made at these sessions, but they can become a source of fun and even musical inspiration. Skilled musicians will be able to take someone else's 'mistake', and turn it into a musical idea. The ideas can flow, and young musicians can learn how to have the confidence to try new things in an environment created just for that purpose. Many musicians can often end up working with the musicians they meet at jam sessions, with many young musicians being 'discovered' by experienced players who heard something they really liked. Along the way, young people can learn that their own, as well as others' mistakes, are an essential part of not only their musical journey, but life itself.

Nikki Yeoh is a pianist who has been influential in the London jazz scene over the last 20 years. She has benefitted greatly from attending and playing at many jam sessions:

The Tomorrows Warriors jam session (formerly the Nu Troop jam session) at the Jazz cafe on Saturdays (early 90's) was where I met musicians, heard my contemporaries and eventually jammed with Courtney Pine for the first time. Visiting international musicians would often turn up so we all got to meet and play with the greats, ranging from Wynton Marsalis, Gonzalo Rubalcaba, Lonnie Plaxico, Steve Coleman...the list goes on!! Even though I was terrified I got up on stage and jammed. My career took off after meeting Pine, and if it weren't for this jam session who knows how I'd have got my foot on the ladder. As a result of me sitting in at the jam session with him, he called me to be in his band!'

It takes a lot of confidence for many children to go and play at a jam session for the first time, especially if they don't know anybody there. However, as a parent, if you can provide the initial support and push, the more they expose themselves, the more people they will meet, the more they will learn and the more fun they will hopefully have. Not only will their ears, technique and overall musical perspectives improve, but also confidence and social skills, through the interaction with other people and fellow musicians.

Professional Musicians

Not so long ago, the only way to be able to talk to a professional musician, would be to go to a concert, jam session, and hope to meet them afterwards. These days it has become much easier to communicate with musicians via Twitter, Facebook, Instagram, or any other social media platform. By talking to or following musicians your child admires, they may have the possibility to ask questions and learn directly from the person they have always wanted to meet. When speaking to some professional musicians, many of them can recall conversations they had with inspirational individuals that either kick-started their own careers, or encouraged them not to quit. Given the opportunity, many musicians are willing to take a few minutes to encourage young musicians or their parents, who are bold enough to approach them and ask for advice. Many musicians will also tweet or post words of encouragement online.

Of course, there are many musicians who you may not get the chance to see or directly contact. Thankfully, icons like Jennifer Batten, Dave Grohl and Sheila E., have given in-depth interviews at different stages of their careers, which are available to stream, download or buy online. Interviews with musicians who are no longer with us, such as Prince or Frank Zappa, are also available to watch or listen to. These interactions, whether virtual or physical, can be a source of inspiration to a child, which can benefit them for the rest of their lives.

<u>Principle #5 - Explore Your Options</u>

There are many options open to your child regardless of budgets or your own knowledge. Exploring these options can open up amazing opportunities.

♩ ♫ ♪

7. Thinking Outside The Box

Stay committed to your decisions, but stay flexible in your approach
- Tony Robbins

Speak to an accomplished musician or teacher, and they will often tell you that practising scales and arpeggios are an important part of learning an instrument for many different reasons. Scales help to improve technique, dexterity and understanding of tonality and harmony. On some instruments, practising scales can also help to improve tone, strengthen your embouchure and the other muscles needed for a child to play their instrument. After practising scales to pass exams or a teacher dictating the importance of scales to improve technique, many children can become disillusioned with the practising of scales and arpeggios for months on end. The same goes for practising long tones, finger positions, stretching, and etudes with a metronome. Perhaps when many children become disillusioned with practising their instrument, understanding the larger context of what practise is for, is key to keeping them engaged.

Middle C. Crotchet. Db. Quaver. Forte. Staccato. These are all words and terms which form part of many musicians' vocabularies. They are terms which describe the way music sounds, and help to explain music in its written form. However, most of these terms are abstract and only apply to music. When we use the term middle C, we are merely attaching letters to a frequency produced by a physical object, which produces a sound. The letter D, instead of being the 4th letter of the alphabet, can signify a note, a key or section of a piece.

Western music theory uses many words from different languages to describe sound, and to instruct performers on how to play what is written. Words such as *crescendo*, *diminuendo* and *staccato* are all Italian, while other terms are often borrowed from French and German. Many children who start to learn an instrument at a young age are still learning to read fluently in their mother tongues, let alone learn seemingly random words in a different language! In order to learn to read music, children are often instructed to look at the notes on a page and learn how to match those lines and dots to where they should position their fingers, or adjust their embouchure (depending on the instrument). If many adults struggle with learning these concepts, it is no wonder that children can feel frustrated.

We often learn music by input; brand new concepts, shapes and sounds are introduced to us, and we are instructed to try and understand them. This unfortunately comes with the fear that without learning these concepts, we will never be good musicians. Since we all grow up singing songs, clapping and dancing, why not use the music, language and concepts we are already familiar with as the starting point, rather than matching new tunes to new symbols and foreign words?

Extraction vs Input

When teaching someone with no prior experience on an instrument, teachers usually assume that they need to fill their students' heads with as much knowledge about the instrument and music as quickly as possible. Many teachers rush to teach quavers, semibreves, clefs and key signatures, while neglecting to take the time to help their student understand the music they already know and are familiar with. We have all been surrounded by different types of music from the day we were born. We are able to sing, clap or dance, which suggests that we all have the ability to process the sounds we hear, respond to those sounds physically, and explain how they make us feel.

Over months and years, people who learn how to play an instrument, learn how to reproduce the sounds they already know, and by doing so, learn to mix and match to write original music. There are some exceptional people, like the savant Derek Paravicini, who can play note-for-note whole pieces after hearing them played once. Other musicians can compose whole symphonies in hours, transforming what they have in their minds into beautiful pieces of music for all to hear. Learning by extraction rather than by input, is all about understanding what is already inside of a child's head, understanding the environments they find themselves in, and helping them make sense of it. In other words, taking songs or elements of music that a child already knows and likes, and using that to teach them exactly the same things that can be learned from traditional beginner's books and classical methods.

As we have already explored, one of the reasons why children quit playing their instruments, is that they become bored. Whether that results from unrealistic expectations, bad teaching or merely developing different interests, when there is no fun involved for children, there is often no motivation to learn and improve. By analysing and teaching songs children already know, children may not become bored as quickly. It not only enables a child to process the information quicker, but it allows the teacher to go into detail slightly faster. It is the difference between telling a child that the first note of the tune *Aura Lee* is a C, or explaining that the first sung note of the song *Let It Go*, from the musical *Frozen* is a Bb. Which one would be easier for a child to remember and understand?

One of the biggest hits of 2015, was a song called *Hello* by Adele. It was the first song to sell over £1million in digital sales and the fastest song at the time to reach 1 billion views on YouTube. It contains the basic elements of a pop song, including a melody, a bass line, drums and vocals, which means that the song can be adapted to be played by many different instruments and in many different styles. Knowing that many children have a general idea of at least how the chorus sounds, what can you teach them through this one song?

The melody can be listened to, played using an instrument and read from a score. The notes can be copied by hand and explained, thus allowing a child to learn note names, rhythms and the conventions of western notation at the same time. On a harmonic instrument such as a guitar or piano, a child can learn how to play the basic chords of the chorus (E minor, C major, G major, D major). These chords may not even have to be explained at first. Just by using their ears, children can copy the phrasing and timing of those chords. The chords can then be explained in terms of their harmonic functions, and the song can be played in all twelve keys, which would help to teach a child about different key signatures, scales and how they interact. What other exercises can we do with this song?

Play the melody	Identify the different sections of the song (chorus, verse, bridge, etc)
Write the melody out on manuscript paper	Play in a different style (reggae, gospel, classical)
Understand what key the song is in	Identify the vocal techniques used
Identify what instruments are playing	Explore what production techniques were used (reverb, echo etc)
Play/sing the melody and bass line	Identify the production techniques
Play the chords (depending on the instrument)	Chords and their inversions
Write out the chords	Background of the artist(s)
Understand the chord inversions	Understand the style and history of the genre

Understand different articulations (legato, staccato, etc)	Play in all 12 keys
Reharmonise	Improvise over the chords

Depending upon the level of a child, some of these exercises will be more beneficial than others. For example, a simple analysis of the chords in the song can aid the understanding of how songs are written, which can help a child to start to write music for themselves. By learning an instrument, the hope is that children can start to create by themselves and begin to experience music, rather than merely understanding what all the lines and dots mean. Many top musicians may still struggle with some of these exercises, which proves that there is always more to learn.

We should not underestimate the power of learning something which we are familiar with. When confronted with a problem we have real interest in, the amount of time and effort we put into it will be very different, compared to something that we have no personal connection with.

Playing The 'Wrong' Way

Is there really a right or wrong way to play? Do you have to learn how to play all scales and arpeggios in all keys? Is there a definite blueprint, only one technique, or are there merely accepted conventions? Do these ideas about how to learn and play an instrument put many children off?

Techniques are just ways that people have been approaching a particular task for decades, or even centuries. As history has shown us, change is not only inevitable, it is essential. New techniques have had to emerge in music pedagogy, to keep up with the change in music, science and technology. Different cultures from around the world, have different approaches to the same music and instruments, each no better or worse than the other (depending on who you speak to!). The way an Indian carnatic violinist holds a violin, is completely different to the way a western classical musician does. The tonguing style used by saxophonist Wayne Shorter, is different to how saxophonist John Coltrane, articulated his notes. The difference in these techniques does not make one musician or genre better than the other; it is simply a testament to the innovation, experimentation and invention of many musicians and cultures. Many musicians are regarded as innovators because they were able to make their disabilities or differences work for them. They turned their mistakes, or disadvantages into advantages.

Often, beginners will try to emulate what they see or hear and their mistakes are quickly and sometimes harshly, pointed out. A child's viola may be out of tune, fingering position may be off, or a myriad of other things which do not look, sound, or even feel quite right to a teacher. As much of a child's first experiences are visual, the aesthetics of performance can alienate or entice them. Children can often feel like they are under pressure to sound and look 'professional', from their first lesson, as opposed to being allowed to be themselves, make mistakes and develop their own style. Sometimes, students need to see the unconventional enigmatic performer, the opposite of the tuxedo wearing, well-postured and poised classical musician, in order to see the worth of their ideas and abilities. They need to be aware that there is not one right way to learn, perform or compose.

A piano player who does not have the 'right' posture?
Keith Jarrett

Classical musicians who play pop music?
2Cellos

A drummer who combines different time signatures together?
Chris Dave

A musician who plays more than one instrument at a time?
Joey DeFranceso

A musician with a disability?
Evelyn Glennie

A musician who makes and plays their own instrument?
Roy 'Futureman' Wooten

A singer who uses their body as part of their performance?
Gretchen Parlato

A musician who dresses unconventionally?
Thundercat

Virtual Teachers

Norman Clarke is one of the most accomplished British gospel organists of his generation, but to get to his level of proficiency, he did not have the luxury of downloading videos from the Internet. The raw gospel sound he wanted to learn was based in America in the 1980s, so he flew to New York and spent weeks in various churches, talking to and recording some of the top gospel musicians, like fellow organist Butch Heyward. On his return to London, he spent hours and hours listening to and transcribing those recordings on tape players, which meant that precise forwarding or rewinding was almost impossible. Nevertheless, he was able to become so proficient that when the Platinum selling and Grammy-nominated musician and producer, Travis Sayles came to London, Clarke was able to play with the visiting choir with ease.

The Internet has fast become the predominant source of learning for many different skills. Specifically when it comes to music, many websites have been created which help people learn how to play a specific instrument, song or style of music. This ranges from websites which list chords for songs, Skype (often used to give lessons remotely) and YouTube which hosts many tutorials, lectures and masterclasses. Millions of videos have been uploaded by people who show viewers exactly how to play a song, by giving a close-up view of their fingers or instruments, while explaining each note or chord, step by step. The videos are often free, are accessible 24/7 and you can pause and rewind anything you want, as many times as you like. It is no surprise that many musicians use YouTube as a learning source and often report that sites like YouTube are a main reason why they became so proficient. It is one of the greatest sources of free musical knowledge, and is used by professional musicians to promote themselves, as well as beginners to show the world what they can do and the progress they make.

Professionals such as pianist Jamal Hartwell and guitarist Andy Crowley, have uploaded many tutorials over the years. Founder and CEO of *Hearandplay.com* Jermaine Griggs, has reached thousands of people all over the world, with online videos and instructional DVD's for a range of different instruments.

'The Internet has opened up a wealth of information and knowledge for children learning musical instruments and much more. Finding the genre of music that piques their interest and allowing them to freely explore videos available on YouTube and other music learning sites, will ensure they remain interested in the pursuit.

Many children lose interest because they cannot relate to the music being taught and performed. Undoubtedly, there is immense value in studying the music of yesteryear and it will take discipline to remain focused. But for long term retention, allowing the student to create their own music (which relies on an understanding of music theory), experiment, pick out musical elements by ear, study performances on YouTube, learn production and technology, among other things, will shift the focus from something they must do into something they love to do.
Oprah said it best: "Passion is energy. Feel the power that comes from focusing on what excites you."

Many people have learned so much from YouTube for one simple reason: because they learn what they want to learn. Learning from YouTube cuts out many expectations, time pressure, money and travel time. It also contains specific and constantly updated information, e.g. how to play the latest Ed Sheeran song on guitar. During the process of learning an instrument, what the student wants to learn can often change. One day, it may be a Led Zeppelin riff and on another day, it may be a jazz standard. The Internet gives a child complete control over what they want to learn. A child wanting to play *A Stairway to Heaven,* can learn straight away, as opposed to being told that they must first learn how to read, learn scales and arpeggios.

Thanks to sites like YouTube, Vimeo and Instagram, the anyone can now post their own progress online and receive objective feedback from complete strangers. The sense of achievement and self-esteem which can come from likes and positive comments, can help to encourage children in some cases, more than a teacher could. Children can also feel a sense of pride when they upload their original music and share it among their friends. This social involvement in a person's musical journey, is an element of learning an instrument which has never happened before in human history. The option to earn money from these sites is also now a possibility, with some musicians who post videos of themselves playing, earning six figures a year from doing so. There are also an increasing range of masterclasses available on demand, which feature world class musicians breaking down complicated techniques and detailed insights into their learning and creative processes.

Technology has also made it possible to give and receive one-to-one lessons on Skype, Google hangouts or other video messaging platforms. Various websites can tell you if a musician you admire is offering lessons, and there is a possibility to learn from them without leaving the comfort of your own home. Not only does this give a child an amazing opportunity to be taught by a great musician, but offers a chance to establish a relationship, get to know a professional musician's present and past struggles, as well as their inspirations and dreams. For teachers, this resource is becoming invaluable, as it allows greater flexibility in scheduling, as well as the spread of their teaching philosophy and methods to places and countries hundreds of miles away. Being able to buy DVD's of masterclasses and clinics from current top working, professional musicians, or even access live performances on the Internet, means that the ability to learn from the best has never been easier in the history of music. These resources can be used in conjunction with music lessons, or for the casual learner, who wants to learn at their own pace.

Apps

There are many apps available which can help a child to learn their instrument. Devices which may have been difficult to carry, delicate or expensive such as metronomes and tuners, are all available to download (mostly for free) on various platforms. Apps are being developed which 'listen' to you play a certain piece of music, and are able to give you feedback about tuning, timing and dynamics. Others will generate pieces, allowing you to have an endless supply of sight-reading material. Some focus on helping their users to read music by giving exercises and tests on note names, and asking users to tap the rhythms they see on screen.

As technology continues to improve, companies such as ABRSM are converting their sheet music and exam supplement libraries into digital formats. As time goes by, apps and other software will overtake physical books as the predominant form of learning an instrument.

Increasingly, apps are being used to compose and write music. Kendrick Lamar's tune PRIDE was produced entirely on an iPhone in 2017 by 19 year-old Steve Lacy. PRIDE was one of the songs on Kendrick Lamar's album DAMN which won a Grammy and went double Platinum in the US (over 2 million tracks sold/streamed).

Principle #6 - There Is More Than One Path

There are traditional methods such as Suzuki, Orff or Kodály which have been around for years. Don't dismiss other methods and activities which can help your child learn and love playing their instrument.

8. Music Lessons = Life Lessons

I would teach children music, physics, and philosophy; but most importantly music, for the patterns in music and all the arts are the keys to learning - Plato

In education, music is often seen as an expendable subject; a luxury, rather than a necessity. The argument is often made for music to be regarded as either just as important, or at least far more important than it is. These arguments often fall on deaf ears, as funding for musical instruments, equipment and lessons are often the first to be cut in education budgets. This represents not just a lack of understanding about how important music and the learning of it is, but also perhaps the weakness of the arguments presented as to why music should have more importance in schools. Much research suggests that music has a very positive impact on maths scores, with some studies showing up to a 20% difference in scores, for those who receive music training compared to those who do not. The problem with all this research, is that this theory does not apply to all people. There are many musicians who were terrible at maths in school, never went to university and could not distinguish Shakespeare from J.K. Rowling. There are many brilliant young mathematicians, who never showed the interest to learn an instrument to a high standard.

meta- *a prefix appearing in loanwords from Greek, with the meanings "after," "along with," "beyond," "among," "behind," and productive in English on the Greek model.* (Dictionary.com, 2018)

Fractions are a classic example of how music and maths interact, with arguments stating that because music is divided into half notes, quarter notes, eighth notes and so on, an understanding of that system will help children learn fractions more effectively. It is hoped that this basic knowledge of fractions will aid the learning of more advanced maths, such as algebra or even calculus in the future.

One of the keys to success in maths, whether one is dealing with decimals or quadratic equations, is the amount of time spent on the problem. Without putting a dedicated amount of time and energy into understanding the rules and concepts of mathematics, even the brightest student can struggle. The idea of dedicating a focused amount of time to solving a problem, does not just apply to maths; the more time spent on a concept or an idea, the better a child can understand and apply. Maybe it is not learning crotchets and minims that enhances skills in maths. Maybe it is the ability to come across a problem and spend the requisite amount of time on it until the problem is solved, that enhances maths and English skills. If a child can practise efficiently, be self-reflexive and progress, the chances of excellence in other endeavours increases. Perhaps it is the meta-skill of perseverance or grit, not the skill to decipher lines and dots and feel rhythm, which is the key link to how music can enhance maths skills. This being the case, the ability to stick to a task can affect any situation a child comes across.

Breaking up big problems into smaller, manageable pieces is one of the most common practise methods teachers encourage their students to use. Instead of trying to play a whole piece or passage at once, by practising a whole, or even half a bar separately and then joining the parts together, children can start to learn that they can break up large tasks into smaller ones. These skills can permeate into a child's life well beyond the time they spend in school, even if they decide not to continue playing an instrument. Perhaps it is time to start thinking about music as a positive end in itself, and stop trying to justify the teaching of music by mentioning its potential benefits to maths and literacy results.

Playing in musical ensembles requires many different skills, which are needed when working with others outside of music. Many children understand the importance of their part in a quartet, choir or orchestra, especially when they forget to bring their music, instrument or piece of equipment to rehearsals. Those feelings of shame and embarrassment can often mean that a child will often make a conscious effort not to forget their things again. Understanding what it means to be part of a group and to take responsibility for your own equipment, are skills which are vital for many jobs and professions.

History and Culture

The most effective way to destroy people is to deny and obliterate their own understanding of their history'. - George Orwell

Learning how to play an instrument does not always have to be about playing, listening, reading or composing. NYU Professor of Music Education Jarritt Sheel has this to say:

'Music, and by proxy art, is the best entry point for many people to learn about other cultures and the implications that art has on history, and that events have on our creative outputs... it gives us opportunities to interact with the past and future, while being in the present wrestling with its implications for our lives worlds and shared reality. It, music, helps introduce and often times inculcate culture, while questioning and reaffirming history's place and our understandings of it.'

Simple historical facts can give a child an alternative understanding of their instrument, the history behind it, and famous musicians. Certain musicians have been extremely influential throughout history, in the realms of politics, sports and business. Musicians like John Lennon and Bob Geldof, wrote songs in the 70's and 80's, which helped to bring the attention of the world to poverty and hunger in different countries. Bob Marley's song, *Zimbabwe*, was written in protest against the Rhodesian government in 1979, and he was invited to perform at Zimbabwe's Independence Day celebrations in 1980 by President Robert Mugabe. One of the most moving songs of all time, *Strange Fruit* was sung by Billie Holliday and uses fruit as a metaphor to describe the lynching of African-Americans in the southern states of the US in the 1930's. The Trinidadian musician, Lord Kitchener arrived in Britain in 1948, and wrote many songs detailing what life was like for him, a West Indian, living in London. Songs like *If You're Not White You're Considered Black,* and *London Is The Place For Me* give us lessons that we can still learn from today.

Music can also be used to learn about, and help to preserve culture. With people migrating to different corners of the world, many traditions and music, slowly become re-contextualised and diluted due to the dominance of global pop-culture. Many young people are born in countries thousands of miles away from where their parents were born, and adopt the dominant culture of their place of birth as their own. This can mean that the bond to their own culture may not be as strong as their parents hoped, which over generations can lead to the loss of languages and traditions. Music can be a vehicle to help children stay in touch with their origins, and help children learn about cultures foreign to their own. That is not to say that a child who studies music will also be an amazing historian! By introducing the music of different cultures to children, they may grow up with a better understanding of the people they interact with on a daily basis in our increasingly multicultural society.

There are many musicians that children can listen to who play traditional music from all over the world. Southern Asian musicians, Ganesh and Kumaresh Rajagopalan, play western classical instruments (violins) but are famous for playing a form of south Indian music called carnatic music. Richard Bona is a Cameroonian bass player, who has played with artists like George Benson and Chaka Khan, but often sings in his native language of Douala. Gilberto Gil is a guitarist and singer, whose Portuguese lyrics often speak of Brazil, its politics and culture. Music can be used as a medium to prevent children from having a narrow view of the world, and to help give new perspectives to those who may only give value to the music they hear played on the radio.

Playing an instrument does not mean a child will end up playing in front of thousands of people, sell millions of records, or pass grade exams. Having knowledge about a clarinet can help children identify and appreciate clarinets, clarinet players and musicians in the future, as well as an understanding of other instruments. It means that they may decide to give their child music lessons when they grow up and have a family. It may even give them another topic to talk about in certain social settings, and help them to form rapport with strangers and co-workers. Some of the most successful people in the world go to concerts and learn about other cultures through music, even if their own musical journey was relatively short. Some of the most successful musicians and music teachers have a heightened sense of society, culture and history because once they begin to explore music, they begin to understand and appreciate the stories, struggles and triumphs that shaped the music they know and love.

Language

Many children begin to learn a foreign language in school but unfortunately, especially in many English-speaking countries, the number of children who leave school being proficient in another language is relatively small. In many schools, children are often taught a foreign language in their native language, and not in the language they are trying to learn. As we know, the use of songs and rhymes greatly aids learning, with the alphabet song being the best example of this. By using music, learning another language can aid the learning of both disciplines.

Listening to music made by French artists in French, can not only give children a different style of music to listen, to but over time, they will slowly absorb the French lyrics. This doesn't mean that they will understand them straight away. In a similar way to how we learn our native language(s), the more we listen to a language, imitate, read then write, the learning of a foreign language can become not only easier, but much more enjoyable.

French	German	Spanish	Arabic
Louane	Johannes Oerding	Chenoa	Samira Said
Camille	Xavier Naidoo	Malú	Amr Diab
Ben L'Oncle Soul	Ina Müller	Manuel Carrasco	Nancy Ajram

These are just a few artists who sing in their native languages and whose music can be used as a teaching tool for children.

Skills For The Future

Eric Marlon Bishop was born in 1967 in Terrell, Texas and was raised by his grandmother. He started to play the piano and led his church choir as a teenager. After completing high school, he attended the United States International University, studying classical music and composition. His musical background allowed him to not only go on to become a two-time Grammy Award-winning artist, but also an Academy Award winner for his portrayal of Ray Charles in the biopic *Ray* in 2004. His musical background enabled him to accept the role of Nathaniel Ayers, a homeless schizophrenic cello player in the 2009 movie, *The Soloist*. Eric Marlon Bishop is an example of someone who has used his music education in a field totally foreign to classical music, composition and choir directing. His role in *Ray* would not have been possible if he had no musical training. Even though being a successful actor does not require a high musical skill, he was given certain roles *because* of his musical skills. Today, we know Eric Marlon Bishop by his professional name of Jamie Foxx.

Others who started their careers as musicians, such as Frank Sinatra, Whitney Houston, Elvis Presley and Barbra Streisand, have all exhibited their talents in film at certain points in their careers. You never know where the skills your child learns when they are young can take them. Maybe they will become a world-famous performer one day but if not, the musical and meta-skills that they learn from music lessons can open doors for them; doors that would have been shut if it were not for their musical training.

Once your child has grown up and is in the process of looking for a job or setting up their own business, how can their experience of learning an instrument help? Even the physicist Albert Einstein was an avid music lover and an accomplished violinist. He did not use his musical talent and knowledge directly in his work, but music was a big part of what helped him become successful and recognised as one of TIME magazine's top 100 most influential people of all time. Elsa Einstein once wrote of her husband Albert that:

'...he also plays the piano. Music helps him when he is thinking about his theories. He goes to his study, comes back, strikes a few chords on the piano, jots something down, returns to his study'. (Pais, 1982)

Einstein used music as a way to re-energise, refocus and relax. It doesn't seem as though he was constantly intent on learning new pieces and preparing for concerts, but he used music as an escape mechanism.

Nathaniel Peat is an entrepreneur who founded the nonprofit organisation *The Safety Box,* and was listed in the 2016 Financial Times as one of the top 100 BME Most Powerful Diversity Executives in the US, UK and Ireland. How has his musical training helped him to flourish in the world of business?

'Music has been amazing in my life. As a youngster having to memorise my scales and arpeggios, it creates a discipline and discipline is the bridge between a goal and an accomplishment. Without discipline you can't achieve anything. Going for my examinations, trying to achieve distinctions as opposed to merits and then using my music as a platform to release stresses. Learning and doing music has really helped me in all factions of my life and it's a great discipline to have acquired [and given me] a platform in other areas of my journey.'

The corporate world understands the role music can play in team building, and employs companies to hold music workshops as a form of relaxation and fun for employees. The company *Creative Volt* has helped companies such as *HSBC, Birds Eye* and *TAM* by holding African, Brazilian and Afro-Cuban workshops, encouraging delegates to play drums together as bonding exercises. It is no wonder that many of the top companies in the world employ live bands for Christmas and end of year parties. The atmosphere and energy generated by live music cannot be compared to a DJ playing records. If large companies know that a few hours of music can have a large impact on adults, the impact on children can be even greater.

We live in a world where we have less and less control over our lives. Many people's jobs are no longer determined by what they originally chose to study. Laws and decisions such as Brexit are voted upon and implemented, which instantly affect our local and global communities. Even Facebook changes its interface without warning. You cannot control the adverts on YouTube, the weather, or the price of oil, but you can equip your children with valuable life skills and strategies through learning an instrument. Spending some time with their chosen instrument and making steady progress, can help children to see how the approaches they take with music can help them to take control over other elements of their lives, and contribute to having positive mental health and wellbeing. Of course this is easier said than done, but once routines have been established, it can have amazing results in a child's life. There are many people, all over the world who find their comfort and escape in playing an instrument, alongside improving their concentration, memory and confidence, all from having music lessons when they were younger.

<u>Principal #7 - Pay Attention To The Process</u>

Help your child to be aware of the many the skills they can acquire when learning an instrument.

9. FAQ's

Study your lessons, don't settle for less.
Even a genius asks questions…
- Tupac Shakur

This chapter contains statements and questions that describe what some children may have felt at one time or another. Hopefully the answers will give some insight into how to help a child on their musical journey.

- **Should I quit? I've been working hard for years but I'm not seeing any results.**

When Michael League started his band almost 10 years ago, he never imagined that they would be playing at locations around the world and receiving the critical acclaim that they currently do. League and his band spent years emailing venues, playing any gigs they could, and often slept in sleeping bags in friends' basements. Snarky Puppy eventually earned their first Grammy nomination in 2013 and their first Grammy win in 2014. Their story goes to show that if you keep on working hard, even if it is 10 years in the making, you can achieve things that you never expected to. Like the stories of Mozart and Handel, the more we learn about successful people, the more we realise that success does not happen overnight.

As she walked onto the stage, hand defiantly placed on her left hip, the audience chuckled and whispered amongst themselves. In an unflattering gold lace dress and hair askew, she looked a great deal older than her purported age of 47. When she said, 'I'm trying to be a professional singer' the camera panned to a shot of a young woman in the audience, whose face summed up the collective thoughts of everyone watching: 'Yeah right'.

When she opened her mouth, Simon Cowell's eyebrows rose, Amanda Holden's mouth dropped and the audience applauded throughout her mesmerising performance. She was given a standing ovation by an audience who by the end of the performance, had learned never to judge someone by appearance on a talent show like this. The video of Susan Boyle's now infamous first X-factor audition, has since reached over 225 million views. Her debut album in 2009, became the UK's best-selling debut album of all time, as well as the biggest-selling album worldwide in 2009. She has since performed for Queen Elizabeth and has duetted with the likes of Donny Osmond and Elaine Paige. She now has an estimated net worth of over £25 million, with two Grammy nominations to her name. What separates Susan Boyle from millions of other talented people? She had the courage to audition and did not quit, even when her dreams seemed unlikely.

- **Will I ever make a platinum selling album?**

There are four main tiers of record sales which tell you, at a glance, approximately how many records have been sold; Silver, Gold, Platinum and Diamond.

How many records do you think you need to sell to be certified platinum? 2,000? 20,000? 1,000,000? Surprisingly, all of the above. Different countries have separate criteria to reach these different tiers, depending on many different factors. If your plan is to become a platinum-selling artist, technically you will only need to sell 2,000 units in Bulgaria, 20,000 in Thailand, or 1,000,000 in the USA. You could be a platinum selling artist in Portugal (at 15,000 units) but no-one in your country may have ever heard of you!

Many successful musicians and singers have never achieved those things or won prestigious awards. Even musicians and bands such as Snoop Dogg (17 Grammy nominations), Björk (14) and Guns N' Roses (3), have never won a Grammy during their illustrious careers. It all depends upon how you personally define success. For some, a successful career could simply be the ability to earn a living from solely playing their instrument. For others, it could mean touring and recording with an established musician or singer. For others it could mean multiple awards, magazine covers and millions in the bank.

• Will I ever be as good as the people around me?

It can be a distinct advantage to be surrounded by musicians who are better than you. With the right attitude, you can learn rapidly and avoid making critical mistakes by listening to the advice and experiences of others. By asking questions, no matter how silly you may think they sound, or by playing in front of people and making mistakes, more experienced musicians will be able to guide you in different ways. By constantly listening to great musicians, you will start to pick up on performance techniques, such as vibrato, dynamics and expression which you can apply to your own playing. Even how they introduce pieces and interact with other musicians and the audience, can be an invaluable source of learning.

Roy Hargrove speaks of his experience one evening, as a 25-year-old trumpet player at a jam session. Saxophonist George Coleman and his pianist Harold Mabern, put the young Roy through his paces.

"He played rhythm changes, I Got Rhythm, and started playing through all the keys. He went through the whole cycle twice. Came back around somewhere in the middle like E major then gave it to me and I'm like "What do you want me to do after all that right?!" But I did what I could... Then after that he played Body and Soul and start going... right in the middle of it he switches from 4/4 to 5/4... then to 3/4 and then to BAM 220 [bpm] like fast tempo, then turns around and gives it to me... It just taught me that I need to go home and practise playing through the keys and also how to play in different time signatures." (irockjazzmusictv, 2011)

The key is to put aside ego and self doubt, and focus on the music. It is easy to listen to a great musician and tell yourself that you will never be able to do what they do. By not worrying about what you can or cannot do, you will be able to focus on what that musician did, how they did it and how it made you feel. One day, others will be looking at and listening to you, thinking the exact same thing.

• **Will I ever be better than other musicians my age?**

'It's ok if you don't practise... but rest assured that there's somebody your age someplace around the planet practising, and if you're lucky you're gonna run into him..and when you run into him don't be angry, don't be jealous.' - *Terence Blanchard* (irockjazzmusictv, 2012)

In reality, if someone has been practising for 10 years longer than you, the chances are that they will be able to do things that you cannot. This does not mean that you should not attempt to better yourself. In school, we work and study in a linear fashion. As we grow older and our grades go up, we learn progressively harder material and have to use longer words and more complex sentence structures. We take exams and become dots on a graph for educators and policy makers to analyse. Copying other peoples work is forbidden. There is always a clear result and a rank and/or grade assigned at the end of a school year.

Outside of school and in the world of music, everything changes. There are no exams, or clear way to determine who is better than who. So, what do you really mean by someone being better than you? The number of records played on, the amount of countries toured in, the amount of gigs in a year, the number of students a teacher has or the amount of views on a YouTube account? All of these things can and have been compared, to determine who is best, or better than the rest. Fortunately in music, copying is allowed - we call it transcribing. You can look at other people's work - we call it sharing ideas. You can play someone else's music - we call it a cover. The sense of competition in music can still remain, but unlike A, B or C grades, there are many more ways in which to measure success.

Music is ultimately subjective. Is she a better singer than you because she can reach higher notes? Is he a better flautist because he can play twice as fast as you? Is he a better violinist because he can double-stop? Arguments could be made on either side for all those questions, but what really separates one player from another? What we are really getting at is individuality.

'Music is your own experience, your own thoughts, your own wisdom. If you don't live it, it won't come out of your horn. They teach you there's a boundary line to music. But, man, there's no boundary line to art.'
Charlie 'YardBird' Parker (Pine, 2011)

• Am I too old to be an amazing musician?
In western society, we often have a fixation on age. If someone has not had a full-time job by 25, or had a child by 35, society can often regard the person as irresponsible, unfortunate or immature. In this microwave society, we want things as fast as possible and with as little energy expended as possible. When it comes to music, if we cannot play a particular song and understand certain concepts by a certain age, or have not sold X amount of records, the first reaction

is often to quit. Consider this: The oldest person to win a Grammy was blues pianist Pinetop Perkins, who won in 2011 when he was 97 years old. Al Jarreau released his debut album at the age of 35 and went on to win 7 Grammy awards. What is the link between all of these people? They didn't quit. Through hard financial times, having children, moving cities and many rejections, they kept going and achieved things that they may not have even have imagined were possible. They did not worry about their age, but instead used their unique experiences to create art that has inspired millions of people worldwide. Don't try to be as good as someone else, just be you.

- **Will I ever sound like some of the great musicians I listen to?**

'If you examine the work of the great innovators in jazz they all had one thing in common: They redefined, edified and expanded the so called jazz language. Sure they might have spent quite a bit of time copying other players and learning tunes and heads and so forth.
But they also did one other very important thing. They spent the vast majority of their time improvising (truly improvising) to find what they had to say as artists. In fact, many had to actually ignore the jazz language of their time. They needed to free themselves from it in order to find a more personal expression.' - Bill Plake (Bill Plake Music, 2011)

There is nothing wrong with wanting to have the skill to sound like a particular musician. Some gigs or projects will call for a musician to sound exactly like another, and having the ability to copy certain nuances, licks or expressions of another musician, can be a useful skill as well as good practise. Aiming to sound like a carbon copy of someone else however, can take away from your own creativity, innovation and ideas. There is always something to learn from other people but by being yourself, there is always something someone else can learn from you.

London-based drummer, Kaz Rodriguez, talks about his experience playing in front of someone that he looks up to:

'I've been fortunate to do drum festivals alongside great drummers and be inspired by them but when they say to me that I've got to show them something I've played, I'm like 'What?' Chris Coleman was one of those guys. He's played for Prince and Stevie Wonder and Chaka Khan. He stood next to me while I was playing and he was like 'You've gotta show me some stuff'. Then I wrote a track for him and we now we feed off each others stuff.'

Kaz travels the world, produces music, sells his tracks and gives masterclasses and clinics. He has also played for artists like Jessie Ware and Aston Merrygold, all the while taking in the many influences he sees and hears on his travels. He is also endorsed by Roland, Zildjian and Tama. He is completely self-taught, so by listening to other great drummers, he has found a way to stand out amongst the crowd. The tracks that he produces, are amongst some of the most covered and sought after tracks online today.

- **I have no time to practise!**

You may have many different things to do, work commitments and various hobbies often leaving you feeling tired. You simply do not have enough time in the day to finish your to-do list, let alone accomplish anything musical. What do you expect from yourself? What do you not have time for exactly? No time to learn *Flight of the Bumblebee* by Rimsky-Korsakov? The bass riff from *Money* by Pink Floyd? Or no time to watch and play along to a YouTube tutorial of a song you heard on the radio?

What do you do to relax? Maybe you scan through social media, watch your favourite series on Netflix, or even a game on your phone. There always seems to be a little bit of time for things we enjoy doing, because they take our minds off tasks we do not particularly like. Can you substitute Candy Crush or Facebook for practising your instrument?

When thinking about either picking up an instrument again, or starting from scratch, it is important to remember that playing an instrument does not now mean that you are trying to become a full-time musician. It does not have to mean 30 minutes of solid practise time every day, or even paying lots of money for weekly lessons. Do not underestimate the fun and relaxation you can have if you set aside 10 minutes a day to pluck, blow or bang on an instrument of your choice. You can start to learn your favourite song with help from the Internet in 5 minutes.

If you are not able to have regular music lessons because of time or money, many teachers may be willing to give lessons once or twice a month (or even less), depending upon your skill level and the goals you've set. A teacher can easily set a months worth of work for you to practise, listen to and/or read. In some cases, teachers can give a lot of theory, exercises and concepts for you to learn, and invite you to call them when you are ready for more. It's important to remember that having lessons every week does not guarantee musical growth. It is all about how much time you put into learning the instrument outside of the lessons.

Playing an instrument is not just about being able to play scales, chords, have expert knowledge of repertoire, tour around the world and make records. Playing an instrument can be a great source of relief and escape from the hectic and stress-filled lifestyles we can lead. When we focus on enjoying ourselves through learning an instrument, the conventional ways of learning do not have to apply. The thing that first captivated us about a specific genre of music, is often the same thing causes us to continue to listen to it, even if we do not play an instrument. If you can get back to how listening to a particular song makes you feel, how it feels to play your favourite song, or lose yourself in noodling around with some scales and chords, time becomes less of an excuse. It could mean playing a song for your friends, or entertaining little children by playing nursery rhymes. All of these things help us to reach into ourselves and enjoy music as a means in and of itself, rather than looking for approval in peer acceptance, record sales or exam results. Focusing on what you enjoy, can often lead you to devote more time to an activity than you think you actually had.

- **I've been practising so why am I not getting any better?**

Your ability to discipline yourself to set clear goals, and then to work toward them every day, will do more to guarantee your success than any other single factor.' - Brian Tracy

Sometimes we confuse practising hard with practising with a purpose. Playing the same scales and pieces in the same way, will produce the same results, year after year. Practising with purpose or practising with a structure, means planning and reflecting on what you have practised, while doing something different each time, until that specific goal you set in the beginning has been reached.

Structured practise is analogous to how we learn maths in school. We start with basic counting and adding single digit numbers, then we gradually move on to the subtraction of basic numbers. We then progress to double digit numbers and include multiplication and division. In a first lesson for example, we might do a few exercises such as: $1+1$, $0+1$, $1+0$, $1+2$. The next day, we might do exercises such as $0+1$, $1+1$, $1+2$, $2+1$, $3+1$. We do not just learn new concepts each day, but we recap old ideas and problems, so that we do not forget the things previously learned. This does not mean that every lesson gets longer, as we don't need to recap every single thing we have ever learned. At some point, we just know that $1+1=2$ and it becomes part of our bank of knowledge. The same goes for bodybuilders. When bodybuilders work out, many write down every single exercise they do. The reason for this, is so that they make sure that they do not repeat the same exercises, at the same weight, every single workout. For them to get stronger, faster or leaner, bodybuilders need to constantly increase/decrease the amount of reps, depending upon the results they are aiming for.

Keeping a log of pieces, scales and exercises, is a good way of keeping track of progress, so that you do not stay on the same scale or piece for months and months. An example of a beginners piano practise log, could look like this:

Day 1:

Exercise	Time (mins)	BPM (beats per minute)	Comments
C major scale (Right Hand)	3	60	Good!
C major scale (Left Hand)	5	50	Good!
C major scale (Both Hands)	5	45	Need to take it slower
Hatikva (song title)	5	-	I need to work on my left hand

Day 2:

Exercise	Time	BPM	Comments
C major scale (RH)	2	65	getting better
C major scale (LH)	3	55	needs to be smoother
C major scale (BH)	5	45	Don't forget thumbs!!!
Hatikva	5	-	still missing the f# in bar 4

Day 5:

Exercise	Time	BPM	Comments
C major scale (RH)	1	80	Good
C major scale (LH)	3	80	Almost there
C major scale (BH)	5	60	Still having problems moving my thumbs quickly
G major scale (RH)	3	50	I keep forgetting the f#
Hatikva	10	60	Bar 11 is sloppy

In this example for Day 1, we can see what was practised, how long it was practised for and what was achieved. In Day 2 we see that for the scales, the bpm have increased and another scale has been added. If we play the C major scale (RH) at 60bpm with no mistakes by the end of Day 1, we can start Day 2, playing the C major scale at 60bpm. If it was perfect, we can increase the bpm to 65bpm for Day 3. We can even write down the new tempos before Day 3, so that there is already a target to work towards. A more advanced jazz player's log might look something like this:

Day 211:

Exercise	BPM	Comments
Minor pentatonics in 4ᵗʰ's	200	E, Ab and Bb are still shaky
All melodic minor scales	160	Only C, G, and F are ok. Ab, Db horrible
All dominant 7 arpeggios	120	good
Diminished 7ᵗʰ arpeggios	120	good - practise them in 3ʳᵈ's next time
Arpeggiate the changes for 'Easy Living'	-	Remember the right diminished scale for the diminished chords
Transcribe the first chorus of Dexter Gordon's Blue Bossa solo	-	Completed the first 8 bars

There is no time allocated for scales, patterns or pieces to learn. This may be because after following a routine for many years and knowing targets, you may know how much time you need for certain exercise. Also, by this stage, practising for 2-4 hours, 5 days a week could be fairly normal. However, an experienced musician might spend all of their time on one scale or pattern, rather than trying to practise different things for an equal amount of time.

This is one reason why very few people reach a high level of expertise in any given field. It not only takes time, but a passion for what you are doing. There is no way you would spend that amount of time every day on something you really did not like, when the options of seeing friends, playing computer games, or even sleeping are available.

Having a practise log written out in this way can also help a teacher prepare for lessons. Many teachers will be able to hear in the first few minutes (or just by body language) if their student has not practised. By seeing a practise schedule, lessons can become more efficient and effective. Having the discipline to be self-reflexive and methodical can determine how successful a musician becomes. Director of Jazz Studies at Ohio State University, Professor Shawn Wallace has this to say about discipline:

'Professional musicians these days have to be able to perform, teach and write music in order to survive, and because it is so difficult, you have to prioritise and have specific goals. You can't waste time! Natural ability is a good thing, but having a lot of natural ability with no discipline, has the same effect as having not much natural ability. Those with discipline but no natural ability will always outproduce. Discipline is the great equaliser.'

- **How can I find a good teacher?**
   When considering the purchase of a car, house or even a mobile phone, an incredible amount of time, energy

and money can go into finding the right one for you. Most people buy with a view to keep for years, confident and hopeful that they will get the best out of their investment. In many ways, a teacher is also an investment. You hope that they will be teaching your child for a reasonable amount of time, and that their service during that time will enable them to learn and grow as a musician and as a person. If that is the case, why not approach finding a teacher in the same way you would when buying a car or a house? Even though you cannot show off your music teacher to friends and family in the same way you might after buying a car, the benefits of taking the extra time to find the right teacher for you or your child can be very important. Similarly, not taking care and ending up with the wrong music teacher, can incur damaging results for a child, and can affect how they see music and learning an instrument in the future.

Performing a quick Internet search is usually the quickest way to locate a teacher. You can narrow down searches in engines like Google or Yahoo, by entering in your town, city, or even just your postcode, with keywords like 'music teacher' or 'music lessons'. If you already know the instrument your child wants to learn, that will also help to increase the accuracy of a search. There are also many agencies and websites which contain databases of music teachers. They encourage teachers to upload their details, so that you as a user, have the luxury of viewing their uploaded pictures, videos, qualifications and experiences, as well as nationally-recognised police checks. In some cases, you will also be able to see where a teacher is located, so you have a clear idea of how long travel might take prior to contacting them. Some teachers will require you to come to their house or studio, while others will be happy to travel to you, depending on the instrument being learned, price or your preference. If you aren't much of an Internet user, the telephone book still holds tutors' information, although services like those are fast becoming predominantly online and app based, to cut down costs and for speed of use.

Referrals are another way to find teachers in your area. Unlike using the Internet where you may be skeptical about testimonials or references, you can learn a lot about a teacher from someone who has personal experience. Whether at work, school, or the gym, asking someone if they know of a good teacher, is an easy way to gather first-hand information to help you make an informed decision. You will be able to learn more about a potential teacher's mannerisms, strictness and demeanour whereas online, negative attributes can be framed differently, or left out entirely.

Asking musicians themselves can reveal certain things that a musician will value and know about other musicians, which a non-musician may not appreciate or understand. Similarly, if you were to ask another music teacher, they will have a different perspective on the strengths and weaknesses of another teacher that they know.

Another good thing about referrals, is the sense of accountability. When you ask a musician about their opinion on a teacher, or even for them to recommend one, you can be sure that they will not recommend someone who they feel could not teach properly. After all, if the person does not turn out to be a good teacher, you will have every right to complain about the recommendation to the person you asked. If the person you asked is considered a friend, they should be willing to recommend the right person for you or your child.

It is important to remember that many teachers can have a hard time trying to find students, especially if they are undergraduates or new to the area. Contacting a university or college with a music department, can also be a good place to ask. Professors may be able to recommend a student to you, or forward an email to any relevant music students. It may be worth contacting conservatories, where the standards of musicianship may be higher, and institutions may have more of an interest in helping their students find work in the music industry. However, it must be said that whether someone is finishing their masters in Music Pedagogy at a conservatoire, a first-year undergraduate studying pop music, or a freelance musician, that is no real indication as to whether they will be an effective teacher for your child. There will be many teachers who look good on paper. They will have degrees and various diplomas. They may have attended some of the best conservatoires and universities in the world. Some may have recorded albums, or toured internationally. It is important not to settle for a teacher just because the search may be taking longer than you thought it would. Location, price, references and experience, are just a few things to take into consideration. The right teacher will be worth a bit of extra money, or a few more miles in a car. Maybe they do not have years of experience, maybe they lack a degree or are charging a lot of money. The right teacher over time, will become much more than a teacher to you and/or your child. They can become mentors, heroes and even lifelong friends.

- **Can I make a living in the music industry if I'm not very good on my instrument?**

Think about when you listen to a song. You hear musicians playing and/or singers singing, but there are many other people involved, without whom the music would not sound like it does. Jobs which the music industry depend on include:

- Mixing Engineers
- A&Rs
- Lecturers/Teachers
- Booking agents
- Composers
- Producers
- Live Sound Engineers

- Music Therapists
- Music critics

There are many people who do not play an instrument to a high standard, or maybe even do not enjoy performing in front of others. They love music but are not actively pursuing a career as an artist or performer. They are happy to be a part of the music-making process, and are an essential part of the finished product we all enjoy.

A few minutes' walk from the seaside in Brighton, you will find one of the best independent woodwind repairers in the UK. Rupert Noble does not play an instrument, but that has not stopped him from being the trusted repairman of some of the UK's top woodwind players. His attention to detail, patience and expertise has helped many woodwind players to achieve the sound they wanted from their instruments.

- All is fair in love and songwriting - Norah Jones

What do the songs *I Want It That Way* (Backstreet Boys), *I Kissed a Girl* (Katy Perry), *Domino* (Jessie J) and ...*Baby One More Time* (Britney Spears) have in common? One man either wrote or co-wrote all of these hits. With 58 top ten hits[2] to his name, Max Martin is one of the most successful songwriters of the last 25 years. Even though he is not well

---

[2] 58 in the UK, 51 in the US

known for playing an instrument, his skills as a producer and songwriter are highly regarded.

Other people have retained their love for music and incorporated it into their careers outside of the music industry. Bill Cosby famously wanted to be a jazz drummer before he started a career in stand-up comedy in the early 1960s. He incorporated music into his stand-up routine and was able to use his platform to feature prominent musicians like Art Blakey, Tito Puente and Stevie Wonder on *The Cosby Show*. There are also people who have reached a high level of musical skill, and have gone on to have careers heavily influenced by music. Even though Tim Minchin has received a Tony award and a Grammy nomination for his work on the musical *Matilda,* he is well known as a comedian whose routines often feature him behind the piano, providing a soundtrack to his comedy. One of his most popular bits, is a song in which he plays in the key of f but sings an f#. Of himself he says,

'I'm a good musician for a comedian and I'm a good comedian for a musician but if I had to do any of them in isolation, I dunno.' (Angryfeet.com, 2009)

• Do I have to learn to read music?

There are many well-known and accomplished musicians who cannot read music. People like George Benson, Sir Paul McCartney and Sting, are renowned for not being able to read music, but have built successful careers nonetheless. Sting earns approximately $450,000 ($1,200 a day) a year for writing the mega-hit *Every Breath You Take*, all without being able to read or write music notation. How is that possible?

What these musicians can do, is use their ears to learn how to play, and take the time to replicate exactly what they heard. When they play their original music with other musicians, they will often sing or play what they want the other musicians to play, as opposed to writing down the music for them to read. They may even surround themselves with people who can read and write music, who then serve as a bridge between them and other musicians. Their ears and technical ability do what their theoretical knowledge does not allow. They may even record themselves singing the parts they want, and direct musicians to follow those recordings. Sound engineer, Rob Hoffman, describes an encounter with Michael Jackson in the studio:

'One morning MJ came in with a new song he had written overnight. We called in a guitar player, and Michael sang every note of every chord to him. "Here's the first chord, first note, second note, third note. Here's the second chord first note, second note, third note" etc. etc. We then witnessed him giving the most heartfelt and profound vocal performance, live in the control room through an SM57. He would sing us an entire string arrangement, every part. Steve Porcaro once told me he witnessed MJ doing that with the string section in the room. Had it all in his head, harmony and everything. Not just little eight bar loop ideas. He

would actually sing the entire arrangement into a micro-cassette recorder complete with stops and fills.' (Jones, 2014)

A musician who is able to read music notation, may be able to teach in more detail, correct errors in musical scores and sight-read chord charts. Ken Burton is a British composer and conductor, who leads the London Adventist Choral and was appointed choirmaster for the Marvel box office hit *Black Panther.* He says:

'It's essential - and I have always advocated - that musicians have the dual ability to understand the code in which the language of music is written, as well as developing the skill of playing by ear. By ear helps retention and overall natural delivery and expression; however, the ability to read means one can achieve a lot more. Reading is a necessity for working in certain areas of music. Naturally, one needs to be a highly skilled and experienced reader in order to play professionally in an orchestra (both classical, and jazz), conduct, and also do complex compositions. In my own work, reading has enabled me to do a lot more, and certainly a lot quicker. Recording session work, for example, has been achieved a lot quicker through the ability to read the score. I've also worked as an accompanist, which often involves not just reading, but reading at sight. It's important to remember that notes are merely symbols to communicate what was in the writer's mind in the first place. The system of notation has evolved over the years to what we use now. I've worked with people who have developed their own system of code, be it numbers, or little symbols; systems which make sense to them, and

enable them to navigate through their careers, so even if the sight of hemi-demi-semiquavers scares you, it's useful to develop some method of recognising some sort of code which can help you to do more than the next musician who relies purely on ear, demo recordings, and lots of repetition in rehearsals. My advice is always: develop both eyes and ears simultaneously.'

If you can carry a conversation and express yourself in a language, you will be able to function comfortably in many situations. If you can write and read in that same language, it becomes an added bonus, and will open up new possibilities. The same goes for music. If you have the opportunity to learn how to read music, it will only help to increase musical opportunities and in some cases, accelerate learning.

- **Will I be able to enjoy playing my instrument one day?**
One of the most important elements of music is fun. As we saw in Olivia's example, once she stopped having fun, she decided to quit. Nursery school children are encouraged to play and explore as a way to learn about their environment. By applying the same ideas to music and music lessons, children can also benefit in the same way. When developing any skill, there are times where repetition and encouragement are needed, but if there is no fun at all to be had, those efforts may amount to nothing.

Learning an instrument can sometimes be boring and tedious. Hours and hours of practising alone is a one reason why many people decide to quit. It is not easy to stop checking various social media accounts to pick up an instrument and play through scales and arpeggios. Having an idea of how fun it can be to engage in music and where it can take you, can help encourage those who are struggling with practising and going to lessons.

Mark Crown is a London-based trumpeter, who plays for the band Rudimental. After years of practise and hard work, he has graced stages all over the world. In his career so far, there are two highlights that stick out for him:

The first one was [being the] guest soloist for the Wynton Marsalis Lincoln Center Big Band. They came over for London Jazz Festival and I was chosen to solo with them, which was a huge experience. The second is currently being a part of Rudimental. Playing trumpet in a big band that travels the world is fun. I've been to many countries (such as India) which I probably would've never been to if it wasn't for touring.'

Learning and fun do not have to be mutually exclusive. Some people find it fun to play along to their favourite song. Some find it fun to see how fast they can play a tune. Some find it fun to pretend they are playing a Mendelssohn violin concerto. It may look funny or sound strange, but as long as they are enjoying the sound and feel of their instrument and connecting to their instrument physically and emotionally, they should be allowed and encouraged to do so.

• What is the 10,000 hour rule?

You may have heard of the 10,000 hour rule which was popularised in the 2008 book *Outliers: The Story of Success* by best-selling author Malcolm Gladwell. The initial research undertaken by K. Anders Ericson, states that it takes approximately 10,000 hours of dedicated practise, to become world-class at any cognitively difficult skill. What it means to be world-class in a discipline such as music, without having quantifiable measurements, is difficult to define. In general, high levels of mastery will usually be recognised by awards or by critical acclaim.

If a child starts along their 10,000 hour journey at the age of 5, with 2 hours of practise a day, 10,000 hours could feasibly be achieved by the age of 19. Of course, there are many arguments against this theory, one of the main criticisms being that 10,000 hours cannot be regarded as an exact number, but rather an approximate amount of hours, or even a rough period of time (10 years). What is certain, is that with dedicated practise over an extended period of time, many musicians have been able to give exhilarating performances and compose powerful and inspirational music.

'You can tell the history of jazz in four words: Louis Armstrong. Charlie Parker.' - Miles Davis

Charles Parker Jr. (known as Charlie Parker or Bird) was born in Kansas City on August 29th, 1920. He started playing the saxophone at age 11 and in his early teens, began learning about jazz improvisation and joined his school band. In an interview, Bird said that for a period of 3-4 years in his teens, he practised for up to 15 hours a day! That equates to approximately 19,000 hours of practise by the age of around 22! (15 hours x 365 days = 5475 hours x 3.5 years = 19163 hours). Those hours of dedicated practise resulted in Bird's collaborations with Dizzy Gillespie, Thelonius Monk, Kenny Clarke and others, with him being regarded as one of the pioneers of the bebop movement in the 1940s. Bird died at the age of 35 and has since been recognised as one of, if not the greatest and most influential saxophonist of all time.

It is important to note that not many people are able to achieve the level of expertise we are talking about. To be able to be dedicated to a task enough to achieve that level of mastery, sacrifices have to be made, as well as overcoming the obstacles of a myriad of other uncontrollable circumstances.

Whether we like it or not, the family a child grows up in, what they are exposed to and their socio-economic background, play a large part in their successes and failures. A person who is able to reach this level of expertise will often use every waking moment in the pursuit of their dream. It may come at the expense of other interests or hobbies they may have. It may mean spending less time hanging out with non-musical friends. It may mean doing no after-school activities and relatively poor academic work. For older musicians, it may mean less time spent cultivating meaningful romantic relationships and more time away from family and friends.

Even by achieving 10,000 hours of solid, focused practise and being surrounded by the positive influences and opportunities, that is not enough to determine whether that a person will win awards or sell millions of records. The concept of 'luck' or 'right place at the right time' plays heavily in determining success. In *Outliers*, Gladwell writes at length about how the people we regard as genius', such as Bill Gates or Steve Jobs, are the products of many circumstances, from being born in the right year, right place, right family and right peers, in addition to having the drive and focus to constantly improve and learn new skills.

Others argue that one can achieve proficiency in far less time, by being very specific about the skill required. For example, a world-class pianist will often be very knowledgeable about the genre they play and about their instrument. They will often know the exact differences between pianos, have extensive knowledge about the history of their instrument and composers, and understand the most intricate aspects of music theory. By isolating exactly what you want to achieve, some argue that it is possible to become a world-class funk trombonist, by studying great funk trombonists like Fred Wesley, and focusing on the few techniques and information necessary to achieve a specific goal. You may not be able to read music, know any theory or the history of funk music, but you may be able to sound like some of the best funk trombonists in the world relatively quickly. It all depends on exactly what you want.

Principle #8 - Question Everything
Even the best musicians in the world have questions. Encourage your child to ask questions and enjoy finding the answers together.

10. The Ideal Scenario?

Olivia is a typical 8-year-old. She enjoys playing with her toys, although she will happily spend hours playing games on her mum's phone. She is doing well in school, gets told off for talking too much and thinks that boys are yucky. She has an older brother named Timothy, who has weekly drum lessons and also plays in a band at school. Olivia likes playing with her brother's drumsticks when he is not looking, hitting anything in sight, sometimes including Timothy.

When she cannot use his sticks, she will clap, dance and hum along to some of the songs that her parents play at home. Her parents observe Olivia trying to sing along to Spandau Ballet's hit *Gold* and encourage her to sing it at every opportunity, especially when other people are around. They buy her a little toy microphone and record her dancing and singing as much as they can. They love seeing her happy, so much so that even though they do not particularly like certain songs on the radio, they turn the volume up when Olivia dances and sings along.

Olivia's parents decide that when she is old enough, they will give her music lessons, as it is clear that she has a passion for music. In the meantime, they buy her a small keyboard, which they allow her to play whenever she likes. They also buy a beginners book for her, even though they have no idea how to read music. Sometimes when Olivia has gone to bed, her mother will learn a few notes, partly to help Olivia and partly because she never had the opportunity when she was younger.

By the time Olivia has her first lesson, she can already recognise some notes and can play through a few of the songs in the book, which surprises her new teacher. Her teacher spends the first lesson listening to Olivia play and asks her questions about the music she likes to listen to and sing. They break into an impromptu song, with Olivia amazed that her new teacher can play one of her favourite songs. Olivia is clearly excited about her music lessons and her new teacher. When they arrive back home, she jumps straight onto her keyboard and plays and sings until it is time for bed. Even though Olivia's mother has dreams of her daughter one day becoming a lawyer, the excitement and joy that these music lessons are bringing Olivia is worth the money she is paying. Olivia's mother is sceptical about Olivia pursuing a career in music, but she is happy to see Olivia enjoy learning an instrument. She pays close attention in lessons and continues learning about music and possible careers, so that one day she can hopefully give Olivia some informed career advice.

Olivia and her brand new keyboard are inseparable over the next few months and she makes rapid progress, playing and singing songs that she already knows and attempting tunes like *Freré Jacque* and *Twinkle Twinkle Little Star*. Because she is still young and her teacher understands the fickle nature of many 8-year-olds, she includes elements of dance, singing and watching videos to keep Olivia's interest. Her teacher realises that the keyboard may not become the instrument she decides to pursue as she gets older and wants to foster a love for music, rather than narrowing her focus so early.

Even though Olivia's mum is happy that Olivia is learning quickly, sometimes hearing Olivia play her favourite song over and over again on her keyboard or watching the same videos online, can become annoying. She speaks to the teacher about this and they come up with a plan to try to expand Olivia's listening. Putting aside their own personal taste, Olivia's parents start playing a range of different music in the house and car, ranging from reggae, to piano concertos, 1920's big band swing and gospel. This has a tremendously positive effect on Olivia, but unfortunately there are still times when she does not want to practise.

Her parents and teacher all understand that her school studies need to come first, so they make a conscious effort to keep her lessons relaxed and certain expectations low. They can already see how she is blossoming as a musician and agree to increase the intensity of her lessons gradually in accordance with her school work. Her knowledge of music theory is increasing and her ability to pick out melodies from songs that she hears is improving too. Her parents can start to hear that her experimenting is gradually turning into her own melodies and little bits of improvisation. One of Olivia's favourite things to do is to play through her first ever piano book as quickly as possible, which helps her to realise how far she has come. The noise that Olivia generates in the house does not improve as quickly as her parents had hoped, but instead of telling her to turn down or stop, they decide to soundproof Olivia's room by blocking the gap under her door with a roll of old towels whenever her practise sessions become too intense. As Olivia gets better, she occasionally enjoys playing her little compositions with Timothy on drums. She dreams of the day when she can perform with a full band on some of the same stages she has seen in many of the videos she watches.

Olivia continues to progress and after some time, she plays a version of *Thinking Out Loud* by Ed Sheeran at a school concert. Her parents are so proud of her achievement. They smile at her obvious love for the music and later that night, show her some of the first footage they ever took of her playing the piano. As a treat for this performance, Olivia's parents take her to see the musical *Wicked*. Olivia is blown away by the whole show, especially by the piano parts she could hear. After consulting with her teacher, her parents buy the official piano reduction and CD for Olivia, even though they know the music is a bit too advanced for her. Olivia is overjoyed when her next lesson begins and her teacher pulls out the book from the musical she had just seen!

As time goes by, Olivia begins to get involved in many other activities after school, in addition to music lessons and her homework. She does gymnastics, swimming and extra tuition every week, so she does not have the time to practise everything her teacher tells her to. However, she still plays the piano and has now mastered many of the songs from the different musicals and pop songs she enjoys. She has accompanied her friends for small performances at school, and they are always telling her how talented she is. She doesn't agree with them because she knows how long it has taken for her to be as good as she is. She smiles every time she receives such compliments and continues to work harder. She even has a few people following her progress online, as the videos her parents uploaded of her playing attract more and more attention.

She has taken a few of grade exams and passed them both, but she finds practising scales and arpeggios boring. She resists and complains when her teacher scolds her for not practising but because of the relationship they have, there is always a level of mutual respect during these exchanges. Her parents do remind her from time to time about the money they have spent on her music education, but at the same time, remind her about the many concerts and musicals they have been to, which have helped to fuel her imagination and inspired her in many different ways.

Now studying at university, Olivia regularly performs at open mic nights and talent competitions on piano or guitar, sometimes plucking up the courage to sing a song or two that she wrote herself. Although she has no ambition of becoming a professional musician in the future, the love she has for music means that it will always be a part of her life. She even started to teach a few young children, which gives her a steady income. She looks back and smiles at the music lessons she had when she was younger, and the ability she now has to earn money from teaching, when many of her friends work in retail earning no more than the minimum wage. Olivia has a wide range of musical knowledge, and the confidence she has gained from the many performances she has given, has permeated into many aspects of her life. She finds giving presentations at university easy, compared to some of her friends who panic every time they have to speak in front of people. Whenever she can, she visits her old piano teacher to give updates about her life at university and learn with no pressure, no expectations but plenty of fun and happiness. She'll never have to say,

'I wish I didn't quit my music lessons.'

Bibliography

Books

Brown, J.D. (1985) Strategic marketing for music educators. Elkhart: Gemeinhardt Co. Ltd

Campbell, D. (1997) *The Mozart Effect*. New York: Avon Books.

Carnegie, D. (1936) *How To Win Friends And Influence People*. London. Vermillion.

Chua, A. (2011) *Battle Hymn Of The Tiger Mother*. New York: Penguin Press.

Deutsch, O. (1966) *Mozart, A Documentary Biography*. Stanford: Stanford University Press.

Gladwell, M. (2008) *Outliers*. New York: Little, Brown and Co.

Pais, A. (1982) *Subtle is the Lord* . 1st ed. Oxford [Oxfordshire]: Oxford University Press.

Pine, J. ed. (2011) *Book of African-American Quotations*. 1st ed. New York: Dover Publications Inc, p.143.

♪

Questlove, Greenman, B. (2013) *Mo' Meta Blues*. Grand Central Publishing.

Rosenfeld, A. and Wise, N. (2001) *The Over-scheduled Child*. New York: St. Martin's Griffin.

Simon, J. (1985) *Handel, a celebration of his life and times, 1685-1759*. London: National Portrait Gallery, p.51.

Stein Crease, S. (2006) *Music Lessons*. Chicago, Ill.: Chicago Review Press.

Journals

Johnson, C. and Memmott, J. (2006) Examination of Relationships between Participation in School Music Programs of Differing Quality and Standardized Test Results. *Journal of Research in Music Education*, 54(4), p.293.

Rauscher, F., Shaw, G., Levine, L., Wright, E., Dennis, W. and Newcomb, R. (1997) Music training causes long-term enhancement of preschool children's spatial–temporal reasoning. *Neurological Research*, 19(1), pp.2-8.

Web Pages

ABRSM. (2016) *ABRSM: Home.* [Online] Available at: http:// gb.abrsm.org/en/home [Accessed 2 Nov. 2016].

Angryfeet.com. (2009) View topic - Interview One - 11th October 2007 at Fagan's, Sheffield, UK *Angry (Feet).* [Online] Available at: http://angryfeet.com/forum/viewtopic.php? p=114473#p114473 [Accessed 11 Nov. 2016].

Berger, K. (2016) *The Truth About Piano Lessons.* [Blog] *Karen Berger, Piano.* Available at: http://karenbergerpiano.com/ category/for-parents/piano-lessons-for-children/page/2/ [Accessed 7 Apr. 2015].

Bill Plake Music. (2011) *The Problem With Studying The "Jazz Language".* [online] Available at: http://billplakemusic.org/ 2011/09/02/the-problem-with-studying-the-jazz-language/ [Accessed 24 Jul. 2015].

Clark, J. (2011) *Marcus Miller speaks on the advantage of reading music & pocket* [Facebook] 16 March. Available at: https:// www.facebook.com/photo.php?v=10150158296310190 [Accessed 8 Sept. 2013].

Daily.redbullmusicacademy.com. (2014) *Red Bull Music Academy.* [Online] Available at: http://

daily.redbullmusicacademy.com/2014/01/james-poyser-interview [Accessed 19 Jun. 2014].

Dictionary.com. (2018) meta. [online] Available at: http://www.dictionary.com/browse/meta?s=t [Accessed 18 Jan. 2018].

GoodReeds. (2016) [Online] Available at: https://www.goodreads.com/ [Accessed 7 Aug. 2015].

irockjazzmusictv (2011) *Roy Hargrove Tradition vs. Innovation.* [Video] Available at: https://www.youtube.com/watch?v=cUbaLwCeri8 [Accessed 12 Aug. 2014].

_____ (2012) *Terence Blanchard- Gives advice to young musicians and shares his thoughts on jazz.* [video] Available at: https://www.youtube.com/watch?v=dk78nCfTR-o [Accessed 4 Feb. 2014].

Jacob Collier. (2016) *About.* [Online] Available at: http://www.jacobcollier.co.uk/ [Accessed 2 Nov. 2016].

Jones, L. (2014) *The Incredible Way Michael Jackson Wrote Music* [Online] NME. Available at: http://www.nme.com/blogs/nme-blogs/the-incredible-way-michael-jackson-wrote-music-16799 [Accessed 11 Nov. 2016].

Leopold, T. (2016) *The making of a prodigy - CNN.com.* [Online] CNN. Available at: http://edition.cnn.com/2012/02/18/living/prodigies-grace-kelly-creativity/ [Accessed 5 Feb. 2014].

Roland (2016) *Roland - Community - Roland Users Group - Brittani Washington.* [Online] Roland. Available at: https://www.roland.com/us/community/roland_users_group/1439/ [Accessed 4 Mar. 2015].

SFGate. (2016) *Playing music can be good for your brain / Stanford study finds it helps the understanding of language.* [Online] Available at: http://www.sfgate.com/news/article/Playing-music-can-be-good-for-your-brain-2594581.php [Accessed 8 Nov. 2016].

TEDx Talks (2016) *Music as a Language: Victor Wooten at TEDxGabriolaIsland.* Available at: https://www.youtube.com/watch?v=2zvjW9arAZ0 [Accessed 5 Mar. 2015].

𝄢

Index

𝄢

𝄢

𝄢

♩:

𝄢

About The Author

Nathan Holder is a musician and writer based in London. He received his masters in Music Performance from Kingston University in 2017 winning the MMus Prize for Outstanding Achievement and tours around Europe playing at various events and functions. He wishes he didn't quit his piano lessons years ago.

Made in the USA
Columbia, SC
02 June 2018